Two Up
Down Under

Ron & Jim Smith

First published in Great Britain in 2017 by U P Publications
St George's House, George Street, Huntingdon, Cambridgeshire, UK PE29 3GH. UK

A CIP Catalogue record of this book is available from the British Library

ISBN 978-1908135681

FIRST EDITION

9 5 7 0 8 1 6 4 2 3

Also published as an e-book by U P Publications

ISBN 978-1908135698

Published by U P Publications
Printed in England by The Lightning Source Group

www.ronandjimsmith.com

www.uppublications.ltd.uk

Two Up
Down Under

By Ron & Jim
Smith

Ψ

2017

Jim Smith

A Canterbury-Pitt comes to Canberra

The previous page shows Jim's New South Wales registered Kombi camper at the 2012 VW Nationals in Sydney.

At first glance, an ordinary Aussie Kombi camper, but a closer look shows that the three badges on the front are from the first three London-to-Brighton air-cooled runs, and that the window of the front loading-bay door has a number of split-screen van-club stickers and a UK tax disc.

To those who know about VW camper conversions, the extra-high-rise pop top could only mean that this Aussie Kombi is a British Canterbury-Pitt camper conversion.

This chapter tells the vehicle's story and how it comes to be an Australian resident now. The story starts in Germany, with the construction of a Microbus for the UK market in March 1967. The vehicle was then shipped to South Ockendon in England, there to have its camping interior fitted to become a VW Canterbury-Pitt Open Plan Moto-Caravan. This involved removing the Microbus passenger seating, cutting a large rectangular

hole in the roof and fitting the pop-top, which originally featured red and white stripes, matching the door awning seen in the first photo.

A full camping interior was fitted, featuring two wooden bench-seats, incorporating storage: a table that could drop between the seats to make a double bed: a water tank and a retractable sink unit.

A fold-out cooker was added to the front loading-bay door and two bunks fitted in the roof.

Additional   storage was added in the form of a large wooden drawer unit over the engine bay, a roomy top-box in the roof, along with necessary supporting bulkhead and additional lighting.

The newly-converted family camper was first registered in August 1967. The first owners spent most of each year in France, where the Canterbury-Pitt acquired a French registration (and a certain amount of French small-change discovered during its later restoration).

During the 'transformation' stage', the van looked like an abstract art installation

In 1986 the camper returned to England and was re-registered as VYY24E, and sold to a neighbour and close friend. For the next 18 months the camper was in regular use as my neighbour, his family, relations and friends, including myself and my family, camped regularly as part of a small camping club.

During this period, it became apparent that Mum, Dad and the three children would not be able to use the VW for too long, as the space available over the engine bay, where the youngest child slept would soon be insufficient. Knowing that a caravan would eventually be needed, I declared my interest in the Canterbury-Pitt, and became the proud owner in May 1988.

The original Cumulus Weiss & See-Blau scheme had been replaced by blue industrial-paint up to the roofline, and a white roof.

While the paint had done a reasonably good job of protecting the body from rot, there were a few little problems, including a number of dents, holes and superficial patches of rust. Initial remedies included replacing the rusted pop-out window frames with aluminium ones and, as a first step, re-finishing in a more attractive scheme.

The various patches of rust were cleaned up and repaired with fibreglass and filler, and the paint scheme was slowly transformed to a cheerful yellow and white, morphing through curiously striking multi-coloured phases as the transformation was taken a few panels at a time, using brush-painting and extensive elbow grease to rub down and polish.

It wasn't long before the vehicle was a highly noticeable colour scheme reminiscent of an airfield air traffic control van. Whilst it was this colour scheme, the single-port 1500cc engine suffered a terminal failure due to ingesting an exhaust valve.

Off to be restored with no roof and no interior – but still a very cool ride in every sense of the words. Once driven to the workshop, the remainder of the mechanicals were removed, and the body shell, progressively taken back to bare metal, was shot-blasted.

This happened near Stonehenge on midsummer's eve, and assistance from the police was commendably quick and efficient, possibly spurred on by the slightly disreputable looking paint scheme.

An engine change to a 1600cc twin-port unit from a scrapyard was soon made and painting completed, to enter the 'We all camp in a yellow campervan' stage, as my two girls used to sing.

This cheerful scheme was retained for the camper from late 1989 to early 1994. During that period the van was laid-up for 1990 and 1991 as the family had moved with work, to the USA, for two years. On returning from the US, family camping with the camping club (and longer camping holidays) continued, with great fun being had by all.

However, the steady onset of rust caused by the British climate, compounded by the use of salt on the roads in the winter, had begun to take its toll. A particular concern was the loading-bay door-sill...

It was acquiring an unhealthy proportion of filler and mesh-reinforced fiberglass. By 1994, action was needed, so the yellow campervan was taken over to Just Kampers in Farnborough for a consultation. The advice was that, notwithstanding the rust in the loading-bay door-sill, the general condition was so much better than 'normal' UK VW buses that I should think about having a full restoration rather than taking a piecemeal approach. More discussion followed – the estimate certainly gave pause for thought.

In the end the family had had so much fun over the last six years with the camper that I decided to go ahead.

The first step was to strip out the interior to the maximum extent while still keeping it driveable. Then the action moved to Fintan, the painter, for restoration to the original colour scheme. The following pictures tell the story of progressive clean-up, and the return of the newly-painted body shell, ready for re-assembly.

The start of the process – removing the remaining mechanicals and running gear.

Then get to work to investigate all the filler. Under here is the evidence of an old collision with a fence post, a huge amount of filler and a floor to straighten. Below: Bare-metalled throughout, sanded and looking like a pewter model, but not the end of the story. All the rust damage has to be repaired, the loading-bay door-sill re-built, a new front valence fitted, and then preparation for painting. Opposite: The body shell back on its wheels to go off to be painted. (photos – Just Kampers)

The new 'old' paint scheme – back to CumulusWeiss and SeeBlau. While all this was going on, the gearbox was being re-furbished, and the interior re-varnished and repaired, where necessary. The most frustrating period was getting the headlining done, but once completed, re-assembly could begin. (photo – Just Kampers)

The 'Miss October' calendar shot

Once Just Kampers had put all the running gear together, it was over to me to re-install the camping interior and, by late September 1994, I was the proud owner of my '28 year-old new car'.

Once put together, one of the first activities was a photo-shoot of the newly-restored camper in front of an autumn backdrop.

This provided the photo that became the October picture in the joint calendar produced by the UK, German and US owners' clubs in 1996. As this was her first appearance in a calendar, she has been known as 'Miss October' ever since.

From the end of 1994 to mid 2002, Miss October continued in use as the family camper, and the typical set-up was with an awning on the side so that a camp kitchen, cooker, wash-stand and crockery storage, could be set up, generally with the table and some chairs.

The camping awning, with its bridging piece across to the gutter edge on the roof continues to be used to this day when camping for more than a couple of nights at one spot. She also attended a number of car shows, typically gaining 2nd place in the SSVC Van of the Year and Restoration of the Year in 1995.

In July 2002 I moved to Australia to take up a position in Melbourne. Miss October was duly cleaned up, emptied of anything that might cause quarantine concerns and shipped in a container to Melbourne, arriving a month or so after the family, in August 2002. After some bureaucracy, RVN442 was registered in Victoria. Owing to certain family aversions to spiders and snakes, and living in the urban sprawl of Melbourne, Miss October had a bit of a pause from camping, but did attend a number of VW Club of Victoria, and RACV events.

After four-and-a-half years in Melbourne, my job took me to Canberra, and Miss October changed identity once again to BA71QQ, registered in NSW and living in Jerrabomberra, which is just outside the ACT.

On arrival in Canberra, I was quickly welcomed into Canberra's chapter of the Sydney VeeDub Club, with whom Miss October has gone on many club events. Highlights include being the club 'Car of the Day' at the 2010 Autofest German car show, coming 2nd in class at the VW Nationals in Sydney, resuming her role as a camper, with a camper-tour over the Easter period in 2012.

This was followed by an 800km each-way drive to the biennial VW Spectacular show, a four day camping weekend at Valla Beach in northern New South Wales and a 13-day road-trip along the NSW - Victoria border. Using the camper in Australia has been a joy. The weather is generally bright and sunny, if not always warm.

Enjoying the English summer sun – out camping with the awning

Above, registered as RVN442, the photo shows Miss October in Victoria at Moorabbin airport, Melbourne.

Below: After the move to Canberra with the author at Captain's Flat, and now with NSW plates - BA71QQ. Following a Club overnight pub run to Captain's Flat, a small mining town up in the hills of NSW.

Easter 2012 camping at the Duera National Forest South of Braidwood NSW. This is the location of the enigmatic but prosaically named 'Big Hole' an 80m circular sink hole in a limestone hillside about 2 km from the campsite.

The country is spectacular, the company is good, and there are endless places to go. On the other hand the old girl is generally the slowest, heaviest, thirstiest and least reliable vehicle when in convoy, and the distances can be daunting.

The pictures that follow show the continuing story now Miss October is based in Canberra. So that's the story of Miss October. I have owned her now for 26 years. In 47 years she has travelled from South Ockendon to Canberra, via France and Fleet.

In colours she has gone from Cumulus Weiss & See Blau through metallic blue; to a patchwork multicoloured quilt; to yellow and white and back to her original scheme. Still going strong, still camping, still with the original fitments.

Below: More rugged camping, Miss October at Yarrangobilly in the Snowy mountains Easter 2012. The camp-site is at about 1400m, or more than 4500 ft elevation, and it was -5C overnight. Top Right: Inside the freezer – waking up in Yarrangobilly. The interior view shows, rather well, the frosted glass effect of being totally iced-up. Right Middle and Bottom: Inside Miss October while at the Honeysuckle Creek campground in the Namadgi National Park, showing the sink, which normaly folds up inside the rear bench seat and, looking forward, the cooker, complete with a camping kettle and original grill pan.

Miss October in the sunshine ready
for another outing with the Canberra
VeeDub Club

MTOW 520 Kg

CLOCK

FLIGHT MANUAL STOWAGE
BEHIND PILOT

OVERVOLT

LOW FUEL
PRESSURE

...or
...tions.
...including
intentional spinning are prohibited.
See flight manual for other limitations.

ON

INTE ON   SS-41

ICOM   A200

ALT
1020
inHg

9 0 1
8   2
       3
6 5 4

10   15
UP VERTICAL SPEED
20
100 FEET PER MIN

Jim Smith

Up Again

The Joys Of Flying Rediscovered

In 2002, I moved from Hampshire to Melbourne, Australia, having won a position in the Defence Science and Technology Organisation.

The move to Australia was a very busy time, with a new job, relocation of the family, and shipping of our goods and effects, including my iconic '67 split-screen Kombi all getting in the way of my resuming my flying.

Eventually, however, I obtained an Aussie special pilot's licence to replace my UK licence and started flying from Lilydale, at the south end of the Yarra valley.

However, there proved to be a number of factors about flying from Lilydale that reduced my enjoyment of the experience.

The initial surprise was the relatively shabby state of the aircraft, which were distinctly tired Piper Cherokees of a number of variants. The worn interiors, partial instrument panels and relatively ordinary radios did not fill one with confidence.

Then there was the training environment; despite being situated with beautiful country just to the north, the preferred flying exercises seemed designed to practice procedures in the crowded airspace to the south, rather than to demonstrate flying skills. A typical sortie would be flying from Lilydale to Moorabbin – probably the second busiest general aviation Australian airport.

A Cherokee at Lilydale – but not one of the ones flown by the author

At Moorabbin one would file a flight plan to Essendon, inside the controlled airspace on the Northern edge of Melbourne and only three nautical miles from the international airport at Tullamarine, followed by departure back to Lilydale. None of this was fun, with continuous radio traffic, the formalities of operating into and out of controlled airspace, late changes of runway, constant attention to look for conflicting traffic and contending with the the vagaries of Melbourne weather.

Probably the final straw was a rejected take-off at Lilydale caused by water in the aircraft airspeed indicator system, which required about 90% of a wet grass-runway to bring the aircraft to a stop.

Although the problem was rapidly fixed, the subsequent flight, creeping around the Lilydale / Moorabbin / Essendon / Lilydale exercise route, in relatively poor visibility and low cloud, was just hard work.

Having abandoned Lilydale as an option, I still flew occasionally on an opportunity basis.

Up from Geelong in my only Tiger Moth training flight to date

Memorable trips included a flight in a Jabiru from Ballarat and a flight in a Tiger Moth from Geelong but, in the end, I could find nothing that suited my desire for a more relaxed atmosphere within a reasonable reach of home.

Four years on, my work took me to Canberra where again, after a period of settling in, I had another shot at flying, this time from the relative quiet of Canberra airport.

Maybe it was just from having been spoilt by all the years of flying the beautiful and much-loved Chipmunk of the Royal Aircraft Establishment Aero Club from Farnborough, but it turned out that having to get an airway's clearance to taxi a Cessna 150 metres from its parking place to the end of the runway did not appeal to me.

The flying was OK, but the formality of everything was not.

There my flying might well have stopped, but for the chance sighting of an internet offer. 'Half-price flying training' on investigation offered a thirty minute or one hour trial-flight lesson at half the normal price.

The offer was made by a company based at Goulburn and, after a bit of thought, I decided to give it a go. Goulburn is about an hour's drive to the north-east from Canberra, but is in a quiet airspace region and might well offer the relaxed experience I was seeking.

A week or two later there I was, up at Goulburn, in January, with my log books, discussing with an instructor my 280 hours of flying experience as a private pilot, and working out the details of the flight.

Looking through the log book, the instructor said to me, "Are you interested in flying in controlled airspace, or are you just flying for fun?" When I replied that I was not at all interested in flying in controlled airspace, he said, "Well in that case you need to convert to a Recreational Aircraft license."

He went on to explain that, by doing so, I would not need a medical as long as I could pass the driving licence medical, I would be able to fly any Recreational Aircraft, which in the Australian context means a light aircraft whose registration consists of numbers rather than starting with VH, with various restrictions on weight, power and so on.

Naturally, I asked what a conversion would involve, thinking that this might involve 5 hours type conversion, appropriate exams and a flight test, and was surprised to be told, "Well, you need to do a minimum of 1 hour's dual, towards which this 1 hour trial lesson counts, and then join the Recreational Aircraft Association before doing 4 hours solo, and then you get your licence."

This was a real surprise. I was potentially within a one hour half-price flight of being able to fly solo, and within 5 hours of being free to fly either by myself or with a passenger.

The next step was to go and be introduced to the aircraft, registered 24-3248, a yellow Skyfox Gazelle, a type I had flown once, more than twelve years previously, from Brisbane's Archerfield airport.

Gazelle 5515 and 3248 at Goulburn Airport

This example certainly looked OK, and we climbed aboard after going through the airframe and engine checks, started up the Rotax engine and taxied out to Goulburn's runway 22 for take-off. The brief was to take off and head broadly south-west into the training area while climbing at 55 kts, aiming to get to 5000 ft, so that a stall could be practised.

Of course, being mid-summer, it was a hot 38C day, and we were about 2000 ft into the climb when I felt moisture on my hand. Looking round the cockpit, I could see a drop of green liquid under the panel in front of me.

I drew this to the attention of the instructor.

It was quickly apparent that the aircraft, although the engine temperatures were still OK, was losing its glycol coolant.

Back to base then, and a return to the hangar to pick up a different aircraft, 24-5515, the green Gazelle, which did look a bit smarter and newer than 3248.

Gazelle 5515, the green one

Off we went again, this time into the circuit.

I had a very lively time with huge thermals, on this very hot day, buffeting the aircraft around. The climb-rate at full power was all over the place – anything from virtually zero to 1500 ft per minute, and I worked hard to fly three good circuits, each one finishing with a very busy approach followed by a smooth landing. At one point I remarked to the instructor, "All this bumping around is the turbulence, not my flying!" to which he was kind enough to reply, "I know … you're managing this at least as well as I would."

Once safely back down after two rather eventful half-hour flights, I was told that if I joined the Recreational Aircraft Association and came back within 3 to 4 weeks I could go solo. I was excited, surprised and relieved all at once. The prospect of being a pilot once again was just around the corner.

A month later, I was back at Goulburn again. Looking at the weather, although the flight school would have let me fly solo, I asked for a couple of dual circuits because of the strong cross-wind, and because I had not flown the aircraft under these conditions. Flying the Gazelle with a strong cross-wind proved to be unexpectedly straightforward, and I experienced a growing   respect for this lightweight but very forgiving little aeroplane.

On the second approach to land the instructor told me to make this one a full-stop landing, and we taxied down to the end of the runway nearest to the flying school, and he hopped out. All I had to do then, was turn the aircraft around, make a radio call 'Goulburn traffic, Gazelle 5515 is departing runway 22, Goulburn into the circuit', line up, open the throttle, and off we go. My first solo flight for 11½ years, which was made after just 1 hour and 20 minutes instruction. I flew a total of 5 circuits, but only landed off 3 of them. One overshoot was due to an aircraft that had landed ahead of me not having   sufficient time to back-track to clear the runway for my landing.

Back on the ground after my first solo flight in more than 11 years

The other was because the strengthening wind was making the approach very turbulent. Climbing out from that missed approach, I decided enough was enough. The next approach was a good one, with careful management of the approach speed and crosswind landing.

I taxied back to the hangar, feeling thrilled to be back in the air again, and surprised by how little effort had been required.

The next step was to complete 4 hours solo flying, which I did by making flights around the outer edge of the local training area, having discovered that one lap plus a circuit or two would take an hour.

Through the whole period, I continued to get to know the aircraft, exploring its stalling characteristics, steep turns and sideslips. I also refined my landing technique, settling on 55 to 60 knots as a better approach speed than the 65 to 70 knots the instructor had told me – probably because of the strong winds on both of my first two flights.

Once I had achieved four hours solo flying, I completed the paperwork and became the proud holder of an RAA pilot certificate, with all sorts of privileges including tail wheel, cross-country, passenger, high performance, low performance, retractable undercarriage and variable pitch propeller.

I must remember to get the appropriate training if I ever want to exercise the latter two.

The next delight was, of course, to begin flying with passengers again, most notably my friend, a colleague from work, Tracey (my first passenger as an RAA pilot), my daughter, Alice, Ron and my partner Kristine.

Of course, one of the greatest pleasures of flying in Australia is the generally good weather.

When this is combined with the spectacular scenery, flying can become a magical experience.

Following Pages: Flying solo around the local area in Gazelle 5515

PILOT CERTIFICATE

Surname:	Smith
Given Name:	James
Member No:	032942
Membership Expires:	31 Jan 2014
Certificate Rating/Approval:	Pilot
Aircraft Groupings:	A
Maintainer Level:	1
Endorsements:	AP HF HP NW PAX R RU TW X

RECREATIONAL AVIATION AUSTRALIA INC   ABN 40 070 931 64 5

The sequence of pictures that follow were taken on a flight from Moruya, NSW, and show the beaches of Central Coast to good effect.

"*Your first Challenge is to sort out a visit to stay with Jim in Australia*"

Ron Smith

Two Up
On The Road

In December 2012, I left my work at BAE Systems after 22 years working on helicopters and then armoured fighting vehicles, following a previous fifteen working on helicopter preliminary design at Westland Helicopters Ltd.

My wife Hilary's reaction to my impending retirement was to tell me that, "Your first challenge is to sort out a visit to stay with Jim in Australia." To make this happen, Kipling's 'six honest serving men', Where, Why, What, When, Who and How needed to be answered.

Starting, as one so often does, at the end rather than the beginning, 'Who' was pretty straightforward – myself and my identical twin brother Jim. He is a senior member of the Australian Defence Science & Technology Organisation, based in Canberra, Australian Capital Territories and living in nearby Jerrabomberra (chosen he said, as much for the fun of making his relatives learn how to spell it, as for its convenience).

At one level, 'Where' was fairly obvious (Canberra), except that we needed to find a core activity, appealing to our mutual aviation interests, around which to centre the visit. 'Why'…

There are many old aircraft still active in Australia and a bit of internet research showed that the National Fly-in of the Antique Aeroplane Association of Australia was due to be held at Echuca, Victoria from 12th to 14th April 2013.

This was to become 'What', the centrepiece of the visit.

The decision as to 'When' determined travel both to and from Australia and to the AAAA event. Arrival in Australia at the start of April would allow jet-lag recovery-time before heading off to the Echuca event.

A return to the UK by 1st May also seemed prudent, this being my 37th wedding anniversary.

The timing of the Echuca visit was down to 'How' we would get there.

Jim said that Echuca was 'within striking distance' of Canberra, being just 256 miles away (about the same distance as between London and Newcastle in the UK). This could just have been a quick car trip on the Friday, staying over locally for two nights and back again on the Sunday.

Jim, however, felt that for the true Australian experience, we should travel in less haste and more style in his 1967 Volkswagen Type 2 Kombi (or split-screen campervan).

Jim has owned the Kombi for some 26 years. It was built in Germany, exported to England and converted to be a Canterbury-Pitt camper. On emigration to Australia in 2002, he brought the van with him and has been using it as an overnight camper and mobile art studio ever since. It has also participated in club events and car shows, including the 2013 rally to celebrate the centenary of the founding Canberra.

His concept was that we should visit some back country Australian tourist attractions, whilst dropping in on airfields, and so on, which happened to cross our path.

Another consideration was that the entire tour should be conducted at a pace sympathetic to the age and performance of the Kombi (and its driver). In practice, this meant driving not faster than 80-90 kph (50-55 mph) and not travelling much more than 120 miles per day.

Jim's local knowledge meant that detailed planning was down to him and for me, the whole trip was something of a 'mystery tour'.

Day 1
The Beginning

Jim's Kombi is a Canterbury-Pitt conversion, meaning that it is fitted out for overnight camping. For on-road travel, two bench seats are provided in the rear on either side of a central table. There is storage, including a freshwater tank, below the seats. At night, the cabin is reconfigured, with the table dropping down between the bench seats to form the base of a double bed with the seat cushions rearranged to form the mattress. Overhead, there is a pop-up awning covering a single bunk on either side, in the roof space.

Some considerable strength and agility is required to insinuate oneself into a bunk. When only two are using the van, these bunks are a convenient place to 'lose' inconvenient items.

Jim's 1967 immaculate Type 2 Kombi at the National VW Show in Sydney

Additional facilities include an internal sink and tap, a two-burner fold-down stove and grill hidden in the door and, at the rear, a pair of storage drawers over the engine bay, hidden below a shelf. An external awning can be fitted outside the double doors, providing an under-cover kitchen and eating space. Despite the remarkable amount of storage available, it was clear that the two of us would have to be careful how much clothing and so on we took with us.

Packing commenced after a ruthless culling of surplus belongings. Jim correctly emphasised the need to be systematic – make sure the things you may need are accessible and keep the rest tidily organised.

Being systematic is the watchword for successful camping in a Kombi.Somewhat to my surprise, we were on the road in good order at about 9 am, heading north through Canberra past Lake George (normally dry, but with some standing water on the far side as we passed).

This route joins the main East West Hume Highway to Sydney a few kilometres short of our initial destination of Goulburn. Jim had recently obtained his Australian Recreational Aircraft licence and his initial objective was to take me, as a passenger, for the first time in many years.

As we headed for Goulburn, it was obvious that conditions were distinctly unpromising for flying, with a strong wind and cloud that got lower as we approached Goulburn. As we left the main road at Goulburn, we stopped for fuel and provisions at the local service area and Goulburn's biggest tourist attraction – The Big Merino. Built in 1985 and re-sited in 2007, the Big Merino, also known as 'Rambo', is made from concrete and is some 50 ft tall. Apparently, it contains an internal gift shop and one can climb up to view the scenery through its eyes. We forbore the pleasure in the interests of getting in the air whilst the weather was at least passable. Friendly airfield staff pointed us in the direction of a small, green, high-wing light aircraft called a Skyfox Gazelle.

After our flight, the instructor took a great photo of the two of us next to the aircraft.

There was some initial difficulty getting it started. Somewhat counter-intuitively, this apparently required that the throttle be fully closed if the engine were to start. The cloud base was too low to get out of the circuit and it was windy, with rain showers threatening. Jim managed just three circuits in moderately turbulent conditions. The lowering cloud meant that we were in and out of the cloud base at circuit height on the downwind leg.

Leaving Goulburn, we drove south for about 40 km through gently rolling countryside with open rolling farm land and wooded ridges towards the village of Tarago.

We were surprised to find that the town was graced with a number of garden sculptures and an impressive mural of horses ploughing on the end of one of the buildings.

The Loaded Dog Hotel (Pub) at which we stopped for lunch apparently has a colourful history, having been associated with the notorious bushrangers Frank Gardiner and Ben Hall. Outside the pub there was a sign advertising 'Anzac Day 2 Up at 2 pm'.

'Two Up' is a nominally illegal gambling game involving betting on whether two coins tossed in the air will both fall with their heads up (Two Up).

It was popular with the troops of the Australian and New Zealand Army Corps (the ANZACs) and the game is played widely using old pennies on Anzac day (April 25th).

The date commemorates the landing at Gallipoli by the ANZACs on 25 April 1915, and the heroism and sacrifice of those troops, which has had a profound impact on how the Nation views itself, and indeed its 'Diggers' to this day.

Inside the pub, there was a reproduction of a 'Wanted' poster for the bushrangers and a slightly inconsistent notice saying that Pizzas were available all day, every day, (except Thursday evenings).

We continued south to Braidwood, which is a typical small NSW country town with wide streets. The old buildings lining the broad main street have large, first-floor balconies.

We stopped primarily to have tea; afternoon tea being a daily routine whose preservation seems to be ingrained in Australian culture.

For tea, we lighted upon a shop which doubled as an extraordinary old-fashioned sweet shop; it was almost a tourist attraction in its own right.

The delights and temptations of the Braidwood sweet shop

Leaving the King's Highway at Braidwood we continued south into 'back country' Australia heading in the direction of Berlang, in the Deua National Park, for our overnight stop at The Big Hole. This took us along empty back roads with the feel of typical 'somewhere in Australia' country roads – dead straight, empty and lined with gum trees.

Autumn was approaching and some of the deciduous trees were turning colour. This trend became more apparent throughout my visit.

About thirty kilometres south of Braidwood, we turned off the metalled road onto the undulating dirt road to the Big Hole campsite, arriving at 3:30 pm. We were the sole occupants apart from some red-necked wallabies. My first experience of setting up the camper awning was a bit frustrating due to unfamiliarity with its components and the required (systematic) sequence.

As we had arrived with a fair amount of daylight available, we decided to head out straight away for The Big Hole. There is a fairly easy path from the campsite to The Big Hole. Having said this, the first thing to do is to cross the Shoalhaven River. Forget bridges, stepping stones and hand rails; all that is provided is a line of rough and rocky stones across the riverbed. The crossing is a very undignified affair, requiring a paddle across the river in bare feet (ow!), carrying shoes and socks as one goes.

Once across, there is a steady uphill walk through trees to a crest, after which there are excellent views of the rolling landscape. The Big Hole itself is some 92 metres deep and about 32 metres across. It is a collapsed limestone cave, or sinkhole and is very craggy and impressive.

The far edge of the Hole looks distinctly crumbly and insecure, so attempting to walk around the rim is not recommended. The sky brightened as we returned.

The evening was marked by the loud, squabbling of sulphur-crested cockatoos as they returned to roost. A splash of colour was provided by an Eastern Rosella parrot that looks as if it has had an accident with a set of primary colour paint pots; its colours including red, white, yellow, green, blue and black. Set in among the gum trees with only the wildlife for company, this was very much a bush camp, although fortunately there was a 'dunny' to meet the essential needs of the visitors. The clocks had changed with the approach of autumn, so we retired, after tea, with the twilight and were in our sleeping bags by 8:30 pm.

Day 2
Big Hole to Canberra and Micalong Creek

We had a surprisingly good night's sleep that first night. Camping is normally a somewhat spartan experience due to uncomfortable sleeping positions and plummeting early morning temperatures. This was, if anything, the opposite. The bed was comfortable, the table underlying the car seat mattresses providing firm, but comfortable support.

Expecting to be cold, we had topped the sleeping bags with blankets. Instead, we woke up to reduce blanket cover at 11 pm before falling back into undisturbed sleep. Undisturbed, that is, until being woken up by an un-ignorable kookaburra alarm clock at 6:40 a.m. I strolled to the river disturbing four or five red-necked wallabies en route whilst Jim prepared breakfast.

Camp breakfast as one of Jim's tours de force reflecting years of experience with the Kombi. Tea, bacon and egg, orange juice, and toast were very welcome, followed by the slightly less enjoyable washing-up, shaving, and so on.

We struck camp, with Jim again demonstrating the speedy systematic stowage of bedding, camp kitchen, plates, cutlery, stores, 'Eskie' (cool box with perishable items) and gas bottle.

As a result we were off just before 9 a.m.

We initially retraced our steps toward Braidwood, stopping only to photograph an unusual tussocky piece of ground that we had noticed on the way in.

In Braidwood itself, we stopped for fuel and started recording how much we were using to help estimate the distance to the next fuel stop.

By then the sky was clearing to signs of a nice day.

Our trip via Goulburn to The Big Hole had taken us south east from Canberra, although our main destination at Echuca was well to the west.

We started our westbound journey by heading back towards Canberra through Queanbeyan, which is the home of a number of notable sportsmen including the F1 driver Mark Webber and the Australian cricketer Brad Haddin.

En route, we stopped at the small town of Bungendore, some 50 km west of Braidwood. The most impressive shop in Bungendore is the Bungendore Wood Works Gallery, which is an amazing art woodworking and cabinet-making shop.

Apart from gift items and art works, there was an upstairs display of the making of the Hannah Cabinet. This is of amazing quality, made over a six year period using 34 different timbers, 4 species of shell and 17 varieties of precious stone with extensive marquetry inlays on its 18 doors and within its 140 drawers. My recollection of the display is that the cabinet is said to be valued at 1.4 million Australian dollars. A search on the internet for details and video of the Hannah Cabinet is heartily recommended.

JEWELLERY FOR BLOKES
EXQUISITE HAND MADE TOOLS FOR WOODWORKERS
JUST IN TIME FOR THAT PERFECT XMAS PRESENT
NOVEMBER 20 UNTIL JANUARY 26,2011

BUNGENDORE WOOD WORKS GALLERY   The Perfect Place for the Perfect Gift for your Special Pe

The entire shop should be an unmissable visit for all who love wood and appreciate fine craftsmanship. We also explored an excellent and labyrinthine second-hand book shop, before adjourning for Morning Tea. As one had come to expect, this was made with loose-leaf tea and was generous, to say the least.

Of all those that we bought during the visit, nothing came close to the Bungendore offering, with a large teapot each containing no less than five cups of tea per person. We were so impressed, we felt that it deserved to be recorded for posterity. I bought a copy of Nevil Shute's *Requiem for a Wren* in the bookshop. Jim said it would make me cry – which it duly did.

A short drive through Queanbeyan took us to Canberra, where we sat for a cheese, tomato and salad lunch next to the 50 m high National Carillon by the side of Lake Burley Griffin. The National Carillon has no less than 55 bells, these being cast at the well-known bell foundry of John Taylor & Co. at Loughborough, Leicestershire, UK.

The Carillon was a gift from Great Britain to Canberra on its 50th anniversary, so it seemed particularly appropriate to enjoy the Carillon in 2013, the year of Canberra's centenary.

Leaving Canberra at lunchtime, we headed for our evening campsite at Micalong Creek, close to Wee Jasper and some 50 km south west of the town of Yass. The route to Yass took us north from Canberra on the Barton Highway. Travelling on this relatively major route, we were somewhat conscious of the speed differential between the Kombi and the other traffic, notably the large commercial 'B-double' trucks, which move goods around Australia's long distances. Jim did his best to maintain speed on some of the uphill gradients, many of which, thankfully, were provided with overtaking lanes. Then, about 10 km short of Yass, we ran into trouble. The engine started to surge at high power and we pulled off the road just after the top of a crest.

We suspected fuel problems and Jim diagnosed the problem as likely to be due to a blocked fuel filter as a result of having dirt in the fuel system.

We drove gently to Yass to pick up fresh fuel and asked at the petrol station if there was a car parts shop in town. The guy serving said words to the effect of 'no idea, mate'. We parked fifty yards down the road to think about our options and then noticed that we were directly opposite the local parts store (duh)!

Following the purchase of a new in-line fuel filter from the store, we set about a rather warm roadside repair.

To complete the job, we needed to buy a set of pliers and finally a small jubilee clip. The repair was completed and we were on the way again by 3 p.m. In all, the fix took forty minutes and cost the grand total of $22.00.

South from Yass on the Wee Jasper road there is a real feeling of country Australia, with a rolling landscape, big skies and gum trees. As we travelled on a wood-lined road, Jim suddenly brought the bus to a halt. "Look behind on your side," he said, "there's an echidna." The echidna or spiny anteater is one of the world's two monotremes, egg-laying mammals, the other being the duck-billed platypus, and hence qualifies as an iconic Australian animal by any standard.

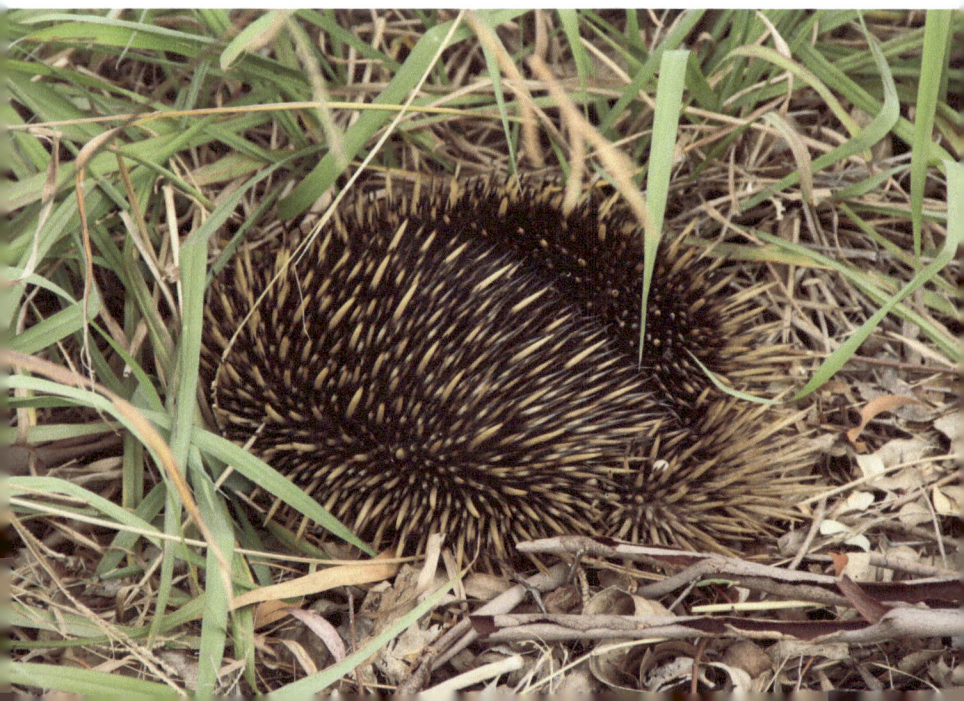

We walked slowly back to the echidna, which had been actively rootling about on the verge when we first saw it. As we approached it hunkered down into its defensive posture, looking like a giant hedgehog with a spiky, black and tan, two-tone, punk-rock hairstyle.

After we crossed the Murrumbidgee Bridge, the landscape became more rugged with signs of convoluted and steeply folded rock strata showing through the surface of the hillsides. We traversed this terrain with an anxious ear to the engine, in case the previous trouble re-emerged. We did not want to grind to a halt away from habitation and in 'no signal' NSW with no mobile phone coverage.

Thankfully, all was well and the engine ran perfectly throughout. After a succession of long climbs and winding descents we reached Wee Jasper – a very small community of about eighty people with a pub and a general store serving its bush tourist visitors. The gravel road from Wee Jasper was fairly rough in places, with short, steep climbs and descents and areas of teeth-rattling corrugations.

We were pleased to reach the grassy haven of the Micalong Creek campsite and to have camp made and the tea on by 5 pm. The site is a beautiful, open, tree-lined area alongside a creek. It has a large playing area and is very family-friendly. We planned to stay here for two nights. Our campsite was, we found, among a large, extended group of camping friends. The ladies of the group all worked at the Pathology centre in Canberra Hospital. They were very sociable and invited us to join them at their camp fire in the evening. As was to prove a common feature throughout, the van (Kombi) was much admired, particularly for the camping interior and its good condition all round.

One of the ladies set the tone by saying that it was 'an absolute ripper'. Her husband had been restoring a Beetle and said that he would look out for the bus at the upcoming VW Nationals in Sydney. The night sky was inky-black and full of stars and we slept to the sound of the rippling stream.

Crossing the Murrumbidgee bridge

Day 3

Day 3 was a day to relax. As we were not travelling on, we took the opportunity to lie in until 9 a.m.

As at The Big Hole, there was a full volume kookaburra chorus and many parrots and rosellas flying around. We took breakfast outside in the shade by the side of the Kombi; the sun was very strong and I needed to stay out of it due to some medication I was taking. In mid-morning, we walked downstream alongside the creek, on a wooded path that was steep in places and somewhat slippery.

We saw plenty of wombat poo, which is very distinctive. It is cubic in shape and is usually left balanced on top of stones and small rocks. The wombats use their scats to mark their territorial boundaries and there is a view that the cubic shape stops it from rolling off the stones and roots on which it is deposited.

We walked as far as the junction of Micalong Creek with Goodradigbee River, before turning round and retracing our steps, arriving rather hot and thirsty for lunch at the campsite.

In the afternoon, we headed back on the unpaved road to Wee Jasper to Carey's Caves.

These caves are formed by subterranean collapses between layers of Devonian Limestone, laid down 400 million years ago.

This results in a complex underground space, which is different from many other river-formed cave systems that are more common, particularly in Europe.

Our guide, Geoff Kell, talked us through an underground geology exhibit.

The samples that we could handle clearly demonstrated just how heavy this ancient limestone is, compared with other sedimentary rocks.

We played boule from the set carried in the Kombi.

On the bumpy, sloping surface of the campsite, various golfing terms such as borrow', 'kick', and 'hazard' sprang to mind.

It was amazing, despite one's best efforts, just how far away from the target you could finish!

The planned evening get-together around the campfire with the Pathology squad was washed out by rain; this was the only heavy rain encountered during the whole of my Australian visit.

Micalong Creek to Gundagai

Day 4

The morning dawned very bright and clear, promising a hot day ahead. We had an early start with a breakfast of muesli and toast, before setting off as early as 8:25 a.m. We retraced our journey through Wee Jasper and the twisty undulating road from there to Yass.

Here we had a short halt for coffee and WiFi access for emails; important as our mother was in hospital in the UK and we needed to stay in touch.

From Yass, we headed along the busy Hume Highway, which runs between Sydney and Melbourne, towards Gundagai. This road is a dual carriageway, which is good in terms of not holding up other traffic, but is generally a less interesting drive.

The distance to Gundagai is about 60 miles, meaning that after leaving Yass at 11:20, we were pulling off at the Gundagai junction by 12:30, giving us plenty of time for local exploration. Gundagai is a small town of around 2,500 inhabitants on the Murrumbidgee River and is widely regarded as a literary and artistic icon of the Australian country town. It is widely featured in Australian writing, poetry and songs and has been the subject of several major flood events in 1852 (killing around 80 people), 1853, 1891, 1974 and as recently as 2012.

We stopped at the Mount Parnussus overview to view the town and its two large, disused road and rail bridges that cross the floodplain, before heading to the local tourist information centre to enquire about local camping grounds.

The tourism office also contained an exhibition display of another tourist attraction, the Rusconi marble masterpiece.

This is a 1.2 metre high model of a complex, multi-tiered 'cathedral-in-miniature', constructed entirely of different types and colours of New South Wales marble. This model was apparently made, without any drawings, over a period of 28 years and contains 20,948 individual pieces.

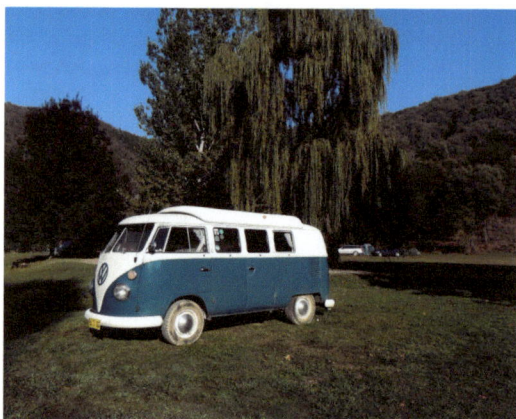

The tourist office directed us to an excellent riverside site almost below the old timber railway bridge and not far from the far end (from town) of the old Prince Alfred road bridge.

The road bridge was built in 1866 and formed part of the Hume Highway until the town was by-passed and a new modern bridge built. In its final 1896 form, the road bridge spans no less than 922 metres, and remained in use until 1977. The 819 metre-long railway bridge is comparatively modern, having been opened in 1903.

A visit to the town end of the two bridges revealed that they were being looked after as 'a managed ruin'. A portion of the road bridge that had been accessible by pedestrians until fairly recently, had been closed due to a deterioration in the condition of the bridge. Both bridges are incredibly photogenic as shown by the accompanying photographs.

Before heading back to the site, we had a look at the Gundagai Railway station, which Jim had previously visited and found full of interest. The station opened in July 1886 and services continued until January 1984.

The building – a type 4 timber standard roadside station – is said to be the largest wooden station still standing in NSW.

It is a tourist attraction full of historical displays, but unfortunately was closed at the time of our visit.

Nevertheless, it made a very attractive backdrop for our own period means of transport.

We had a relaxed evening, but retired very early due to the clocks going forward for the autumn.

Gundagai railway station was still in use when the Kombi was built in 1967

Day 5

Gundagai to Temora

We had an early start, being up, dressed and showered by 7 a.m.

I went off to take some early morning photographs of the bridge, whilst Jim made breakfast.

The Day 5 trip to Temora airfield and museum focused the trip more on travelling across to Echuca and on any airfields, museums and items of aeronautical interest on the way.

This was a very hot day and I was taking great care to use the Factor 50 sun cream and to wear my wide-brimmed and not-exactly-stylish hat.

We had a delay on setting off, as it appeared that flashing the headlights to let trucks know that they could pull in was causing the indicator fuse to blow.

We asked around town for help finding a car mechanic. The first place that we called in on could not help, but thought that the van was an absolute beauty and asked if they could photograph it.

They could, however, point us in the right direction and we were soon in the right place (ironically very close to where we had just stopped for fuel before starting looking for help).

The mechanics offered a set of 10 spare fuses for the magnificent sum of $5, stressing that Jim did not have to buy them all; a typical example of Australian generosity.

Jim bought them all on the principle that it could be hard to find more if he needed them.

Our 75 mile route to Temora took us into flatter and less interesting territory through the dusty medium-sized town of

Junee, which was dominated by grain silos and the railway line, which appeared to be a mainly freight operation.

Apparently (Wikipedia), the town's economy is based on agriculture, the railway and government services (specifically correctional facilities).

Suffice to say that it lacked the attractions of Gundagai.

In Junee, we did some food-shopping, bought ice for the 'Eskie' and then hooked up to a very slow WiFi server.

We were soon pulling into Temora and finding our way to the camping area.

As it was roasting hot, Jim said that he would set up camp and that I should tour the museum, which he had visited many times before.

Temora Aviation Museum is home to many interesting types, which are maintained in flying condition and regularly fly displays at Australian air shows.

The museum was opened in July 2000 and has been a great success. Among many highlights are the only two flying examples of the Supermarine Spitfire in the Southern Hemisphere, the last flying Gloster Meteor F8, and flying examples of the De Havilland Vampire, Commonwealth Wirraway, Boomerang and Sabre, Cessna O-1 Birddog, English Electric Canberra, Lockheed Hudson, North American T-28, and, O-2A and AT-37 Dragonfly.

Whilst walking around the display hangar, I met Quincy, who is a member of the museum staff. After a long chat, I was escorted around the engineering and maintenance hangar and introduced to the Chief Engineer, Andy.

Both were very interested in my *British Built Aircraft* books, which I went back to the bus to get for them. They were hoping to fly to Echuca with the Commonwealth Wirraway and said that they would look out for us, although in the end, they were unable to make it.

Temora is an active airfield and evening flying included an AESL Airtourer 150, a high performance homebuilt F1 Rocket that we saw again later at Echuca and a Regional Airlines Piper Navajo.

A hot day was followed by a spectacular sunset.

At Temora, we were joined late in the day by Alice, Jim's 15-year old daughter, who travelled with us for the rest of the trip.

1940 Ryan STM S2 VH-RSY on display at Temora

This made the camper a little more crowded.

One of the bunks was now needed, nightly, in addition to the double bed down below. We travelled with three on the bench seat in the front, which was a little cosy at times.

On the other hand, we had the considerable pleasure of Alice's company, and an extra pair of hands to assist with the routine tasks of setting up and taking down camp each evening and morning, washing up and so on.

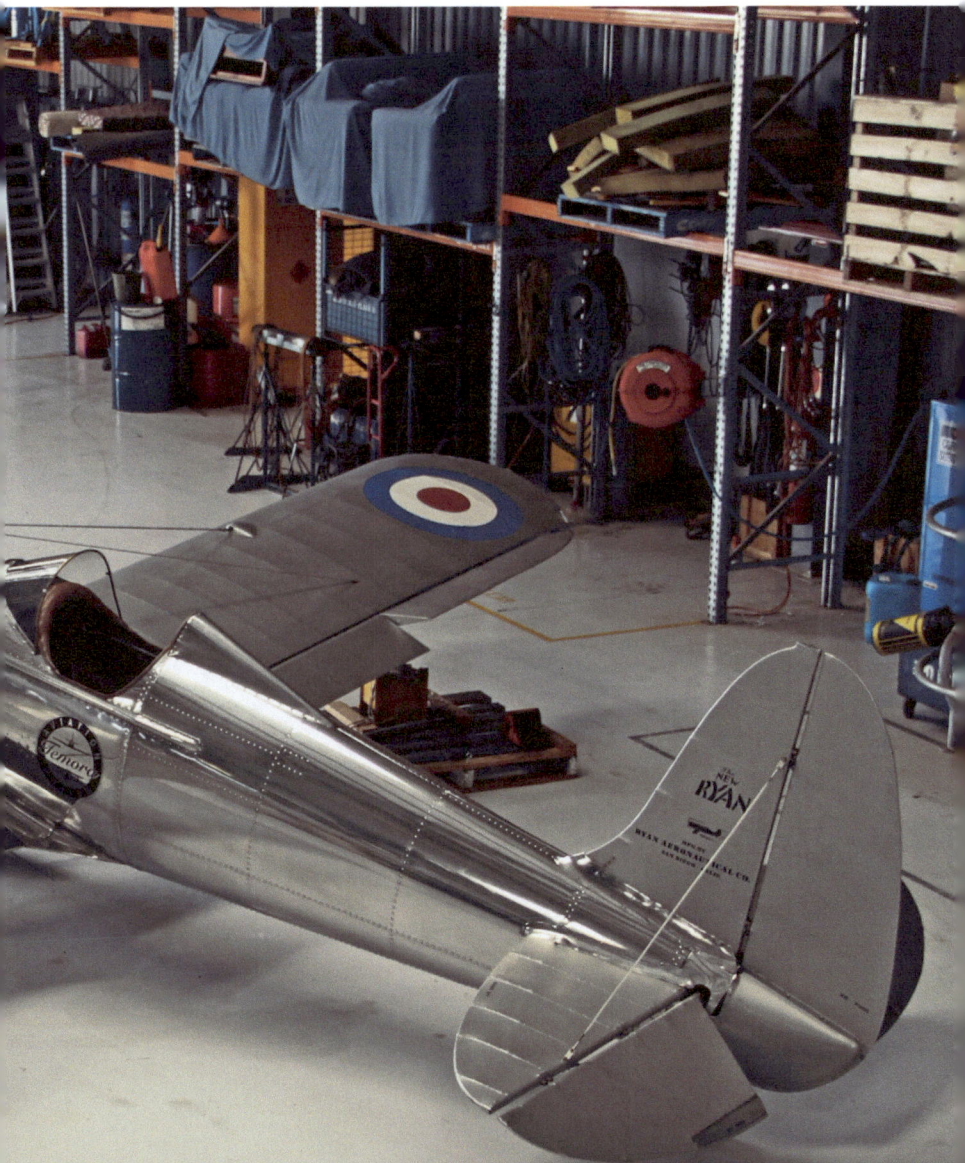

1944 Commonwealth
CA-16 Wirraway Mk 3
VH-BFF

1969 Cessna A-37B Dragonfly VH-DLO in Vietnamese colours

Evening arrival of a Regional Airlines Australia Piper Navajo

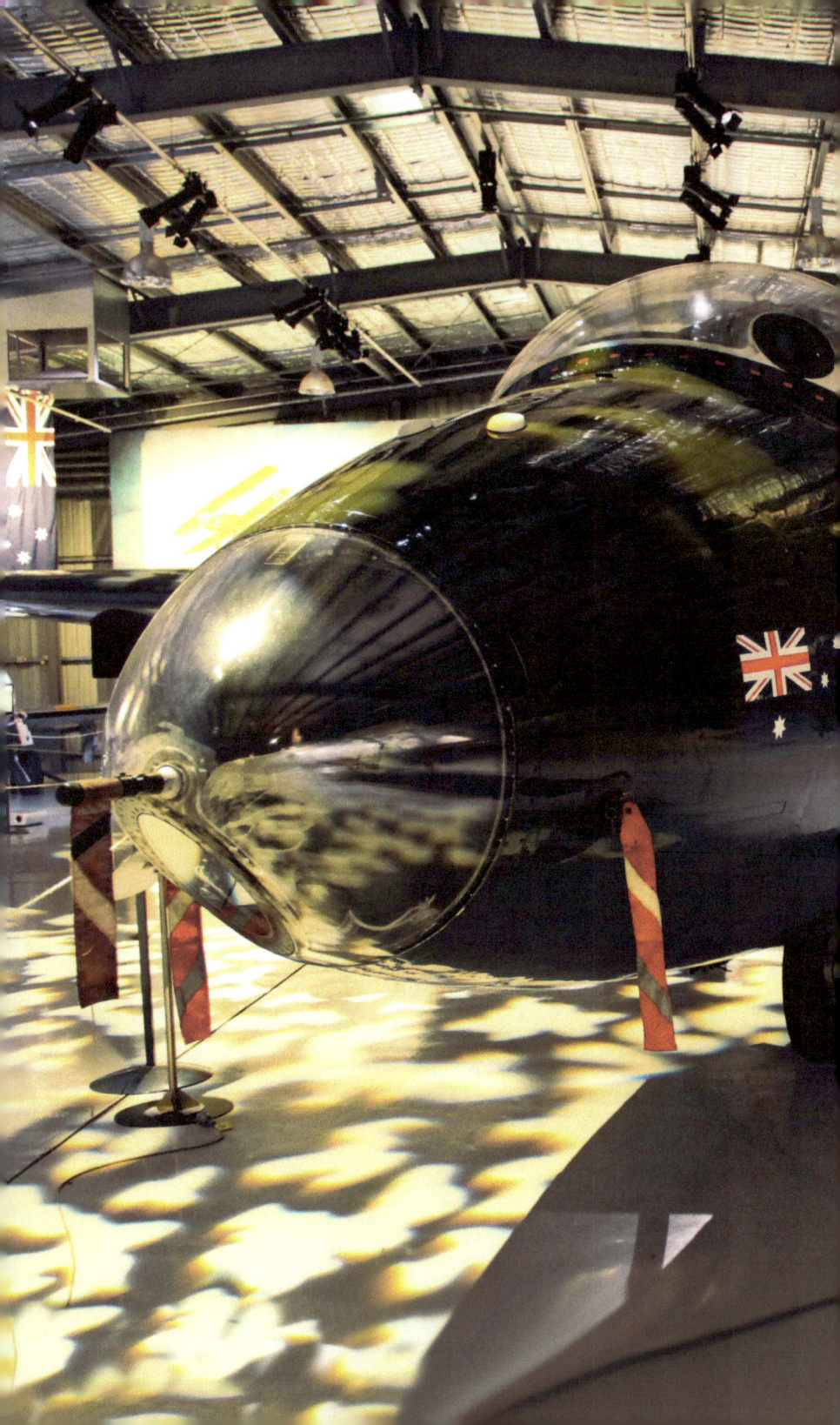

WJ680 VH-ZSQ is one of the last
English Electric Canberras still flying

DAY 6

Temora to Albury via Wagga Wagga

This was a transit day to get us farther south on the way to Echuca. We set off, now with Alice on board, at 0930 on the planned long run (210 km, 130 miles) to Albury, beginning with a necessary fuel stop. When travelling in the Kombi, fuel usage is a constant issue. The Kombi has a small fuel tank, the aerodynamics of a house brick, and is very heavy because of the camping interior, water, food and so on. When one adds to these characteristics the long distances between fuel stations in country Australia, and a somewhat unreliable fuel gauge, keeping track of fuel consumption is an essential part of route planning, and we kept a record throughout the trip. The fuel data showed about 2.5 litres 'lost' per journey, with consumption thereafter of 12.66 litres per 100 km.

For a 40 litre tank, this meant a typical range to an empty tank of 300 km or 185 miles. The route took us to the city of Wagga Wagga (so good they named it twice?), a large town with a 50,000 population, said to be the largest inland city in

New South Wales. At Wagga, we stopped to photograph the de Havilland Vampire trainer, which is displayed on a pole by the roadside, before continuing to the civil airport at Forest Hill, some 12 km east of the city.

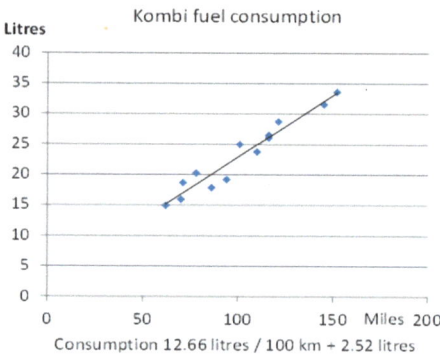

Kombi fuel consumption

Consumption 12.66 litres / 100 km + 2.52 litres

The airport is an RAAF base, which has a civil enclave on the north side acting as the commercial airport. Forest Hill was not a very rewarding airfield for the enthusiast to visit.

It had embraced the modern trend for high fences, with no public viewing area. The apron was populated by a number of commuter airliners such as the Saab 340 and De Havilland Canada Dash 8. On the far side, there looked to be the nucleus of an aviation museum, with an RAAF Aermacchi MB326 jet trainer, an RAN Westland Wessex anti-submarine helicopter and a camouflaged Australian Army Nomad short take-off and landing transport aircraft, all parked out in the open. This area did not seem to be accessible beyond the airport's boundary fence.

We stopped for lunch at a bakery that had lots of appealing roadside advertising as we approached. This was a mistake, as the food was very poor.

De Havilland Vampire on display in Wagga Wagga

Regional Express Saab 340 at Wagga Wagga

Cargo Embraer EMB-120 Brasília

Camouflaged GAF Nomad

(Top) Lake Hume, to the east of Albury, covers an area of 31 square miles when full

(Bottom) The 'lion' rock at The Rock

Items shown on the menu were not available, service was disinterested and the men's room paper towels had run out.

The advertised beef curry pie was little more than a layer of curry powder on top of a beef filling – no apparent effort had been made to make a curry sauce. The establishment invited customers to fill in a feedback form, which we duly did.

In fact, we ran out of space on the front of the card, and had to continue on the back in order to record a total of 8 critical comments.

All in all, it was a triumph of advertising over quality and one of very few disappointments on the whole trip.

We continued past an outcrop called The Rock, which looked like the profile of a lion.

The route took us south on the straight and flat Olympic Highway.

One wonders about the origin of the name, remembering that there is also the Mount Parnassus viewpoint in Gundagai.

Straight, flat roads seemed to be a feature of the Riverina Plain and the Murray River basin, which we were now approaching.

We saw a signpost to another great NSW place name (Burrumbuttocks) and reached the town of Albury at 1430. Albury is another large town, albeit slightly smaller than Wagga Wagga.

The local tourist office was in an attractive house opposite the large Victorian railway station, which looked like a smaller version of Melbourne's Flinders Station.

It has a 450 metre covered platform, one of the longest in Australia.

We followed the office's suggestion and headed east of the town to an attractive and very well equipped site on the shore of Lake Hume, which provides water for irrigation and electricity generation.

Day 7

Albury to Deniliquin

Overnight, we received an encouraging email concerning preparations for the publication of our 'Two Up' memoir.

We were on the road by 9:10 on the way to Deniliquin via Berrigan following the Riverina Highway in a broadly west northwest direction.

After leaving the camp site, we visited Albury airfield, which proved both welcoming and of great interest. The first aircraft we stopped to look at was an Australian agricultural aircraft of a unique configuration.

This is a biplane with a short, stumpy fuselage containing its chemical hopper and two short, separated tail cones supporting the tail surfaces.

The separated tails were designed to allow a vehicle to approach from behind to re-fill the chemical hopper when required.

Known as a Transavia PL12 Airtruk we glimpsed it through a door whilst driving past the back of a hangar.

On asking if I could come in and photograph the Transavia, the chap on the hangar door jokingly said, "Oh, yes …that Transylvania thing."

The Airtruk first appeared in 1965 and, surprisingly, for such an unusual design, 118 were built and the type was exported to several countries.

We met a charming and enthusiastic couple with a restored Cessna Birddog on amphibious floats.

The Birddog is a Vietnam-era observation and Army cooperation aircraft, but is not normally seen on floats, although its relatively high power is well-suited to this application.

(Top) Transavia Airtruk VH-TZZ at Albury   (Bottom) Cessna Birddog on amphibious floats

The owners loved both Ron's books and Jim's Kombi, the wife saying that their family had had five Kombis when they were growing up. Her husband's first reaction to the Kombi was to say, "That's a fine weapon you have there!"

The hangar contained several other interesting light aircraft and it was a delight to meet another pair of evident enthusiasts. They asked if we were headed to Echuca and said that they hoped to see us there.

On the far side of the airfield was a silver Douglas DC-2 wearing the Dutch registration PH-AJU and KLM markings; even though not airworthy, it is an extremely rare survivor. The DC-2, or Douglas Sleeper Transport, was a precursor to the famous DC-3 or Dakota.

PH-AJU took part in the 1934 MacRobertson Air Race from England to Australia and, during the race, made a diversionary landing at Albury in bad weather, before finishing in second place overall in the race.

Preserved Douglas DC-2 at Albury

Only eight DC-2s survive world-wide. Despite being painted as PH-AJU, the aircraft at Albury is a different example, NC13726, previously operated by Eastern Airlines, Australian National Airways and the RAAF. It was erected at the airport as a pole-mounted memorial to the original aircraft's unplanned visit to Albury during the Air Race.

The aircraft was removed from the pole in around 2002 for remedial structural work.

This was a long, hot day on the Riverina, made more frustrating by missing a junction in Berrigan, adding some 25 km (16 miles) to the planned 200 km (125 mile) journey. We got to Deniliquin feeling tired just after 3 p.m. and opted for cabin comfort, rather than setting up and breaking camp in the morning. An evening visit to Deniliquin airport resulted in a fantastic meeting with some agricultural aircraft operators, who were real flying enthusiasts and seemed delighted that we had dropped by their operation. I asked if I could photograph a spectacular-looking and brand-new Ayres S2R-T34 Turbo Thrush VH-HHH. The response was, "Yes, of course. Do you want us to put the engine cowlings back on?"

They asked if we were enthusiasts, or did we have any flying connections and we explained that we were heading for Echuca on a road trip in the '67 Kombi and that we were both aeronautical engineers and pilots. The boss took the trouble to retrieve his iPad from his car to show us film of the newly restored De Havilland Mosquito fighter-bomber flying in New Zealand.

In his view, the New Zealand flying scene was even better for old aircraft than Australia. He particularly recommended Blenheim, Hamilton and Marlborough and said that the Marlborough 'Omaka Classic Fighters' air show, which is held in alternate years to the well-known 'Warbirds over Wanaka' event, was actually the better of the two.

As we left this hangar, I said that we were dropping by the various airfields on our way looking for interesting aircraft and agricultural aircraft were always interesting.

The two chaps looked at each other and then back to us and said, "Have you seen what's in the other hangar?" moving immediately to open it up.

Inside, lit up by the setting sun, were two more agricultural aircraft, a turboprop Air Tractor AT501 and a huge, piston-engined Polish PZL Dromader. The Dromader was impressive, not to say imposing, when seen close to. With a wing span of nearly 60 feet and an engine delivering the best part of 1,000 hp this is one of the world's largest crop-spraying aircraft; more than 750 have been built and the type is also used for water-dropping on fires, some 22 are registered in Australia.

We left, after much admiration of the Kombi, with good wishes ringing in our ears.

Whilst in Australia, we saw eight different types of agricultural aircraft, something one would be hard put to do in the UK.

(Top) Spectacular Ayres S2R Turbo Thrush VH-HHH   (Bottom) Air Tractor AT501 at Deniliquin

The dominant Dromader

Day 8

Deneliquin to Lake Charm via Lake Boga and Swan Hill

Deniliquin (Deni to the locals) is a dusty, flat agricultural town that outsiders might describe as 'bogan' Australian slang for unsophisticated.

It is famous for its 'Play on the Plains Festival', which includes the Deni Ute Muster. A Ute (utility vehicle) has a two-door driving compartment and a loading well area to the rear.

They are widely used as agricultural utility vehicles, but high performance V-8 and customised models are widely available and proudly owned. The town has adopted the name of 'Ute Capital of the World' due to the huge success of its annual gathering.

At the Muster, not only are there a huge number of Utes, but attendees are encouraged to come wearing blue singlets; some would regard this as further evidence of 'bogan-ness'.

In October 2013 a World Record Blue Singlet Count was set by 3,924 musterers in blue singlets. 9,736 Utes attended the Muster, also a record.

To be fair, Deni, outside 'ute' mustering season appeared to be a quiet and civilised country town, albeit having an ongoing love affair with the ute.

By our rough survey, driving through the town, no less than 80% of the cars were utes. Alice was very taken with Deni and indicated she would like to come back when the Ute Muster was on.

A quick getaway saw us leaving the campsite at 8:20 a.m. We made a short stop to photograph the Kombi next to a 'Beaut Ute' on a pole at the entrance to town and picked up more fuel before heading out at 8:50 for Kerang, Lake Boga and Swan Hill.

The latter was the farthest point from home of the trip, being 440 miles from Canberra on the most direct route – that we had not taken – and some 170 miles from the border between Victoria and South Australia.

Ayres Turbo Thrush Kerang Airfield

We entered Victoria by crossing the Murray River from Barham NSW to the settlement on the opposite bank of the river, Koondrook, and continued from there to Kerang. The route took us along the Murray Valley Highway, which was, without question, the dullest road that we encountered. We also noticed that the temperature was higher and conditions notably more humid in the Murray Valley than elsewhere on our travels. Kerang airfield revealed another Ayres Turbo Thrush. This example was not as immaculate as the new aircraft at Deniliquin. The airfield seemed very quiet, with no sign of activity and only one other aircraft visible.

We stopped in the town for a coffee break and a visit to another second-hand book shop.

Our next significant destination was Lake Boga 'the home of the Catalina'. Despite being some 400 miles inland from Australia's east coast Lake Boga was used as an inland maintenance facility for RAAF, Dutch and US flying boats during the Second World War. The Japanese bombing of Darwin in February 1942, with a number of ships sunk and at least 240 people killed, demonstrated the potential vulnerability of military bases, to attack from the air, leading to the decision to use Lake Boga as the 'Number One Flying Boat Repair Depot'. Aircraft supported by the base in addition to the Catalina included the Dornier Do 24 (Royal Netherlands East Indies Air Force), Short Sunderland, Supermarine Walrus and Martin Mariner.

A Consolidated Catalina flying boat is preserved at Lake Boga in a purpose-built building (sponsored by the local Lions Club). The museum and its exhibits are absolutely first class. On entry, we were invited to watch a twenty-minute introductory DVD. This had clearly been thoroughly researched and was made at a time when contemporary film and people with first-hand experience of the base and its operations were still available for interview.

The Catalina museum was a super place to visit, with excellent displays and insightful supporting material.

The preserved Catalina in the superb museum at Lake Boga

Dutch Dornier 24 front fuselage at Lake Boga

From Lake Boga we headed the comparatively short distance north to Swan Hill, for a very pleasant lunch – a platter of local specialities – next to the Murray River, which forms the border between Victoria and NSW.

The restaurant restrooms featured a mirror surround designed to appeal to any 'Ute Musterer'.

After a couple of wrong turnings, we found the Giant Murray River Cod, which is one of the town's attractions. This provided an opportunity to compare the fine lines of the Kombi with those of the Cod. It is perhaps wise not to dwell on the picture that Jim posted on Facebook, saying "Oh my Cod, it's a Kombi".

As usual, we could not resist a visit to the local aerodrome, which was also rather quiet, the main aircraft of interest being a Grumman Ag Cat agricultural biplane and a comparatively rare (in Australia) homebuilt Bushby Mustang II.

From Swan Hill, we headed back south several miles to Lake Charm, to give ourselves a shorter run to our primary destination of Echuca the next day.

Lake Charm provided a most pleasant and quiet camp site on the shores of the lake.

We broke out a pair of inflatable chairs that Jim had apparently had for ages, but never had an occasion to justify their use.

Blowing them up (and subsequently deflating them) without the aid of a foot pump was a nuisance, but was well worth the effort for the rather surreal scene once the pair of us settled down to use them.

A Grumman Ag-Cat crop spraying biplane at Swan Hill

VH-IFE

Day 9

Lake Charm to Echuca

By 8:45 a.m., we were up and about, completing the final pack-up at Lake Charm, getting on the road by 9:20 for the relatively short drive of approximately 72 miles to Echuca.

The area of lakes and lagoons between Kerang and Lake Boga is well known for populations of ibis and has one of the most populous ibis rookeries in the world.

We stopped briefly on the way, at an ibis observation hide, only to find that it was presumably not ibis season, as there were none in sight.

By 11:00, we were at Echuca, looking at the early arrivals for the fly in. This was a gin-clear day of unseasonably hot (30C) weather.

Jim went off with Alice to find a campsite in Echuca, leaving me with one of his telephoto lenses.

I avoided the intense sun by sitting in the club house and emerging from time to time to photograph interesting new arrivals.

When Jim came back with Alice, having set up the campsite and unloaded the Kombi, he borrowed my Canon EOS7D camera, the best we had between us, to take some beautifully composed images of the star arrivals.

Echuca and the Antique Aeroplane Association of Australia National Fly-in was the centrepiece of the trip and did not disappoint.

We were at the event for a good part of Friday and all of Saturday among friendly and hospitable hosts. Day 9 and 10 are therefore largely given over to a selection of our best and most interesting photographs from the event.

This period cockpit interior belongs to a 1947 Aeronca 11AC Super Chief VH-IDH, the only example of its type in Australia. Reflections from the perspex made this difficult to photograph, whether normally, or by using flash. In this case, Ron's stylish wide-brimmed sun hat is being used to eliminate the reflection, providing a curve that nicely follows that of the chrome control wheel.

The weather was good for flying, particularly on Friday, and by the end of our visit, we had photographed 106 individual aircraft of 62 different, mainly older, types, with a mix of more modern and homebuilt aircraft.

A selection of Friday's best images are presented in alphabetical order by type, with explanatory comments, as appropriate.

Avro Cadet VH-AGT landing at Echuca

The Boeing Stearman 75 was built in large numbers during the Second World War as a primary trainer for the US Army and US Navy. Two aircraft came to Echuca; VH-JQY is a 1943 Stearman E75 painted as an N2S-5 of the US Navy.

The Cessna 180 is a popular and highly effective short take-off-and-landing utility aircraft. Three different aircraft flew in to Echuca, with VH-MTF being a particularly immaculate example. A total of 6,193 Cessna 180 was built between 1953 and 1982.

The Cessna C190 and C195 are clean and attractive five-seat high wing cantilever monoplanes powered by radial engines. Rarely seen in Europe, six of the ten Cessna 190/195 registered in Australia flew into Echuca. These types are very much the successors to the Cessna Airmaster series. Production of the 190 and 195 ran in parallel from 1947 to 1954 and comprised around 1,180 aircraft.

The Commonwealth CA-25 Winjeel trainer is an Australian equivalent to the British Hunting Provost. The Winjeel was designed to replace the Tiger Moth and was powered by the 450 hp Pratt & Whitney Wasp Junior engine. Two prototypes and 62 production aircraft were built. Around half appear on the Australian register and, of these, four flew into Echuca.

The DH82A Tiger Moth was Britain's most important primary trainer in the Second World War. The type was also built in Canada and Australia. Six examples flew into the event at Echuca, equal to the Cessna 190 / 195 for the most numerous type to fly in. The Tiger Moth has ideal characteristics as a trainer, being relatively easy to fly, but difficult to fly well.

A rare visitor was a 1937 Hornet Moth VH-UXY. Originally, this aircraft was registered in the UK as G-AEZG, being exported to Australia as VH-UXY in July 1979. Only two DH87B Hornet Moths appear on the Australian Civil Aircraft register.

Another rare De Havilland attendee was the magnificent DH89 Dragon Rapide VH-UTV. Originally built in 1940 for the RAF as DH89B Dominie HG656, the aircraft was sold to New Zealand, before being imported as VH-IAN. It is now painted in the colours of A33-1, the RAAF's first DH89 aircraft.

Three De Havilland Canada Chipmunks flew in. The Chipmunk replaced the Tiger Moth as a primary trainer with the Royal Air Force. It is a popular aircraft because of its delightful handling qualities and its usefulness as an aerobatic trainer. Its enduring popularity is reflected in the fact that no less than 50 appear on the current Australian civil aircraft register. This is an aircraft for which Jim has a particular fondness, having some 180 hours on type, with many cross-country and aerobatic flights completed in the UK before moving to Australia.

The Nanchang CJ-6 is an aerobatic trainer developed in China from the Russian Yakovlev Yak-18. The CJ-6 is preferred by some to the similar Yak-52 due to its flush-riveted construction and its fully retractable undercarriage, which confer less drag than the partially retractable undercarriage of the Yak-52. 16 appear on the Australian civil aircraft register.

The NZAI or Pacific Aerospace CT/4 is an aerobatic trainer developed from the Australian Millicer Airtourer. The aircraft was used as a primary trainer by the New Zealand, Thai and Australian Air Forces. More than 150 were built and 30 appear on the Australian civil aircraft register.

Another aircraft of which only a single example was seen was the Stinson 108-3 Voyager VH-ROA. This   is a relatively   high performance American light aircraft, of which more than 5,000   were   built   in   a number of versions, with small numbers currently flying outside the US. Five aircraft of this type are listed on the Australian civil aircraft register.

In among the vintage aircraft were a number of homebuilt aircraft. There were two examples of the Thorp T-18. Dependent on the engine fitted these are quite high performance aircraft. At least 400 have been built, only 5 of which are registered in Australia.

Warren Canning's Van's RV6 with Jim on board

Vans aircraft are responsible for the design of a range of enormously successful homebuilt aircraft. Eight Vans homebuilts flew into Echuca, 5 RV6 and 3 RV7 models. Jim was given a flight in a Vans RV6 flown by a DSTO colleague Warren Canning. Warren is the son of the late Clive Canning, who built a Thorp T-18 VH-CMC and flew it to Britain in 1976 to the UK Popular Flying Association Rally at Sywell, Northamptonshire.

Jim's flight included aerobatics with a loop (entered from level flight in the cruise), an aileron roll and a barrel roll. With typical generosity, Warren's first words to Jim were, "Hi Jim, great to see you here – let's go flying." Later in the weekend, Warren also took Alice flying, including her first-ever experience of aerobatics.

We retired mid-afternoon to the large, heavily occupied and rather expensive campsite on the bank of the Murray River. Once again, conditions down by the river were rather hot and humid, but the river itself was graced by a number of paddle steamers offering river cruises to the many tourist visitors to the area.

Day 10

Echuca

This day was spent wholly at Echuca. Ron was dropped at the airfield in, thankfully, cloudy and cooler conditions – good for comfort if not ideal for flying and photography.

Jim spent the morning with Alice on tourist activity, before joining up at the airfield later on.

As well as exploring Echuca, Jim and Alice had a very enjoyable river cruise and lunch on the Emmylou paddle steamer.

The cruise along the Murray River allowed a good view of the historic port of Echuca, which used to be an important centre for the wool trade, where bales of wool were transported down the Murray by paddle steamer before being transferred to rail or road transport and taken down to Melbourne for export.

Once back at the airfield, the Kombi continued to attract admiring comments; it seemed that most people interested in older aeroplanes also like to see a 45 year-old camper still being used as originally intended.

As with Day 9, the Day 10 story is a compendium of the best and most interesting photographs of visiting aircraft, in alphabetical order by type and with explanatory comments.

Above: 1951 Auster J/1B Aiglet VH-WAZ. Among the most numerous types at the event were Austers. These were built by Auster Aircraft of Rearsby, Leicestershire, initially in wartime and on through the 1950s. All-in all, Auster built more than 3,500 aircraft, many being exported, particularly to Australia and New Zealand. Eleven flew in, of six different models. One of the variants that is comparatively rare in the UK is the J/1B Aiglet; of 86 built, 72 were exported. Two examples came to Echuca.

Below: The lovely and rare Avro Cadet spent the whole day flying. It was a real delight to see such a rare aircraft operating so busily and an extra photograph is felt to be justified – a sight that one could not see anywhere else.

Above: Another rare highlight was the 1934 British Klemm Eagle VH-UTI. Only two examples remain; G-AFAX in the UK and this aircraft in Australia. The type was built as a touring monoplane with most examples having a retractable undercarriage. First flown in early 1934, 43 were built. Contemporary advertising offered a cruise speed of 130 mph and a top speed of 150 mph. the British survivor G-AFAX previously operated in Australia as VH-ACN and has a fixed undercarriage. Before migrating to Australia, Jim flew a Chipmunk aircraft from England to Holland in company with G-AFAX, so the Eagle was another aircraft with which he had a special connection. **Below:** The 1952 Cessna O-1 Birddog VH-UXX, taking off below, is a military observation aircraft, seating two crew in tandem. Developed from the Cessna 170, it was first flown in December 1949. 3,431 examples of the rugged STOL aircraft were built and it is popular with private owners seeking an entry-level warbird. Three Birddogs came to the Echuca fly-in. These included VH-FXY, an ex-Vietnam Air Force aircraft belonging to Rob Fox, in which Ron had previously flown from Moorabbin to the RAAF Museum at Point Cook.

Above: The 1940 Commonwealth CA-3 Wirraway VH-WWY landing at Echuca is an armed Australian-built development of the North American Harvard. This example was not the one that we had seen at the Temora Museum, but an earlier CA-3 model, the 40th of a total of 755 Wirraway that were built. The Wirraway continued in service with the RAAF until it was replaced by the Winjeel in April 1959. Around 10 examples remain on the Australian civil aircraft register.

Below: A fine action shot of Winjeel VH-HFM stirring up the dust on the taxiway. The Commonwealth Winjeel replaced the Wirraway in RAAF service. Initially entering service in 1955, it remained in use in the Forward Air Control role until 1994. Close up, the type appears to be very solidly built. One of the Winjeels at Echuca, VH-DKK, was in camouflaged Forward Air Control colours, rather than the more familiar training scheme.

An Immaculate DH82A Tiger Moth VH-NWM The Tiger Moth remains ever-popular among vintage aircraft collectors. A search on the Australian civil aircraft register reveals that no less than 186 are registered, although not all of these are necessarily active. All those at Echuca looked in excellent condition. The red VH-NWM, silver VH-AKE and blue/silver VH-AZF were particularly attractive.

Above: VH-UTV (painted as A33-1) climbs away. The timelessly elegant DH89 Dragon Rapide VH-UTV with its fine lines, attracted admiring glances on the ground and in the air. The Rapide was important in the development of regional airlines pre-war in the UK, but its main production success came after it was selected by the RAF as the Dominie wartime navigation trainer and communications aircraft. A total of 730 were built.

Below: One of the most attractive DHC-1 Chipmunks seen, was VH-MCC. This immaculate 1947 Chipmunk is notable for being a very early example, construction number 22 of some 1,292 built. As an early aircraft, this example did not have anti-spin strakes in front of the tailplane and lacked the bulged rear cockpit side windows used on RAF training examples.

Above: Luscombe 8A operating on the recreation aircraft register as 24-5184. Ron was particularly pleased to see a Luscombe 8A arrive, registered to operate on the Recreational Aircraft register. He has owned two such aircraft, one built in 1940 and the other in 1946, and has more than 350 hours experience on the type. Jim now has an RAA recreational aircraft licence that would allow him to fly this type.

Below: 1941 Ryan ST-3 KR VH-RPT A single example of the Ryan ST-3 KR flew into Echuca, this being VH-RPT. The type is closely related to the Ryan ST-M seen at Temora, but has a Kinner radial, rather than a Menasco inverted inline engine. With its polished aluminium, exposed radial engine, wire-braced wings and undercarriage and tandem open cockpits, the type has a definite air of the 1930s about it.

The magnificent American-registered, 1939 WACO AGC-8 NC66206 was our last machine and a real surprise. WACO was noted for fast designs aimed at the wealthy private owner. In car terms, think Aston Martin, rather than Ford Mondeo.

The quality of their products is, perhaps, best captured in WACO's own advertising slogan 'WACO Airplanes: Ask Any Pilot'. The reflective maroon paint and dove-grey leather-upholstered interior was of jaw-dropping quality. The WACO was quite busy flying, but once or twice looked rather 'squirrely' on landing. Any purchaser would need a thorough check-ride with a suitably experienced instructor.

We left the airfield during the afternoon to visit the town for some mild tourism. On our way back out of the airfield, we were delighted to meet the lady we had previously seen in Albury (with the amphibious Birddog), who recognised us and / or the Kombi and wanted to know how we were enjoying the event!

The riverside 'Port of Echuca' area in Echuca is a popular tourist area, with gift shops, restaurants and interesting displays. A horse drawn stage coach provides town tours and the paddle steamers are ever popular.

Jim has been writing children's stories for his grandsons, featuring the adventures of Tuffy and Tippy (respectively a toy tractor and dumper truck). He was very pleased to find a store that represented Tuffy and Tippy heaven.

One of the street displays is of a red gum log buggy, showing a single tree trunk to be pulled out of the forest by a team of bullocks. The 'buggy' itself dates from around 1870 and is made entirely of red gum, including the wheels. The sign on the log indicates that it was cut down in the Moira Forest NSW and is 20 ft long with a girth of 18 ft and a volume of 4,860 super feet.

A super foot is an archaic unit of volume used in Australia and New Zealand for milled timber, being apparently 144 cubic inches, so the volume of the log is approximately 405 cubic feet.

The port area is popular for wedding receptions and one was being held that afternoon in an outdoor restaurant area overlooking the river.

This made for some interesting people-watching, with Alice in particular being very interested in the various fashion disasters on display. Not wishing to intrude, my photography was limited to the going-away car, which was a suitably stylish red Holden Torana with the remarkably apposite number plate 'DOWDY'.

One well-known dictionary definition includes the phrases: untidily shabby; out of date; and lacking in smartness or taste.

An Australian would surely sum this up as 'bogan'.

Day 11

Echuca to Rutherglen via Tocumwal

This was the start of our return trip to Jerrabomberra and from this point on, our objective was very much based on getting as far as possible on each day without over-doing it.

The bus was on the road by 9:30 a.m., with a quick trip to the airfield to see if there had been any new arrivals. The big surprise. in terms of new arrivals, was an Italian-built SIAI-Marchetti S-211 jet trainer.

This aircraft, registered VH-DZJ, had originally been sold to the Singaporean Air Force. 21 ex-RSAF aircraft were sold off to IAP Group Australia in 2009 and VH-DZJ is one of a number on the Australian civil register (8 listed at the time of writing). Built in 1985, it is by no means an antique, but would surely be a welcome guest at any fly-in.

Most of the other aircraft were getting ready to depart, so we felt that we would not miss much by starting our way home. Leaving the airfield at 10:00, we made a fuel stop at Nathalia, before heading off to investigate the Sportavia Soaring Centre at Tocumwal. We had worked for the Sportavia-Putzer company at Dahlemer-Binz in the Nordrhein-Westfalen region of Germany when we were students, and wanted to know if there was a connection with the company, or whether the name was a coincidence.

It proved to be a fascinating visit.

The Sportavia Soaring Centre was no longer active, but there was a glider on the apron adjacent to one of the hangars. We spoke to the gentleman there, who turned out to be one of the world's most famous glider pilots, Ingo Renner.

An unexpected visitor SIAI Marchetti S-211 VH-DZJ

Schleicher ASW-15B glider at Tocumwal with Sportavia hangar in the background

After explaining our interest in the name, Ingo said that he had been asked by Sportavia to participate in evaluation of the new RF5B Sperber motor glider – probably at about the time that we had been working with the company.

He well remembered flying with Manfred Sliewa, with whom we had worked.

Scheibe Bergfalke training glider

Liking the company name, the club had sought and received permission from Alfons Putzer to use the Sportavia name for their business. There was a hangar full of gliders at Tocumwal, including the only two examples of the 17-metre Edward Pascoe EP2, an Australian design. There was also a Schneider Kookaburra, Scheibe Bergfalke and a Caproni CA25 Calif.

Ingo Renner is a four-times winner of the World Gliding Championship and has some 30,000 hours experience – much more flying than most airline pilots achieve in their careers.

He has been Australian gliding champion nineteen times.

  He has been honoured with the Medal of the Order
of Australia (1988) and the Australian Sports Medal (2000).

The only two Pascoe EP2 gliders in the hangar at Tocumwal

Homebuilt Stratus, Tocumwal

Glider advert for Sportavia

The next hangar was the home of an aerobatic school, where Jim rapidly established his credibility by discussing Chipmunk aerobatics and his experience of box-judging at the World Aerobatic Championships. The owner was keen that Jim should come back when there was a competition on. "It's only five hours drive from Canberra; we are always short of judges for competitions."

Jim said that, unfortunately, it was more like two days drive in the Kombi!

Also on the field were a homebuilt Stratus, a Liberty XL2 and a Piper Pawnee Brave. After the airfield visit, we returned to the town centre and had an excellent lunch. The Sportavia club was advertised by a glider mounted on a pole in the centre of town, which was duly photographed.

Our next airfield stop was at Yarrawonga, where a wingless Pawnee Brave sat on the airfield, along with aircraft ranging from microlights to a Cessna Citation business jet.

A Wingless Pawnee at Yarrawonga

We pressed on east, past the spooky, drowned trees of Lake Mulwalla.

Lake Mulwalla was formed by damming the Murray River and has a curious road bridge across it. The bridge has a dip and a bend in the middle.

Apparently, the bridge was built simultaneously from both ends; it only became apparent at a late stage that the two ends were not going to meet – hence the need for the roadway diversion.

We ended our day in Rutherglen on a quiet comfortable site, just back from the main street next to an attractive tree-lined man-made lake.

Day 12

Rutherglen to Tumut via Holbrook

The objective for day 12 was again to get as far as possible, whilst recognising that Jerrabomberra was still beyond reach, being 400 km (250 miles) away. We left at 9:15 a.m. headed west, crossing back into NSW at Albury after some 30 miles. From there, we headed north-east for another 40 miles to Holbrook, photographing a microlight on a pole signposting the road to Holbrook airport.

Holbrook is an interesting town. Despite its distance from the sea, it is the adopted home of the Royal Australian Navy Submarine Squadron. The reason goes back to the First World War, where the first Royal Navy VC of the war was awarded to Lt Norman Holbrook. Lt Holbrook was the commander of submarine B11, which escaped on 13th December 1914 under fire from a minefield in the Dardanelles, where it had torpedoed and sunk an enemy ironclad.

Harassed by torpedo boats and surface guns, the escape required running submerged for some nine hours. At the time, this settlement was named Germanton. A wave of patriotic feeling resulted in the town being renamed Holbrook on 24th August 1915. In 1995, the Royal Australian Navy decommissioned the Oberon-class submarine HMAS Otway offering its conning tower to Holbrook as a memorial. There was a public appeal to acquire more of the vessel and a generous donation by Lt Holbrook's widow Gundula allowed the town to acquire all the surface casing of the submarine above the waterline to use as the final memorial.

Sapphire microlight on a pole in Holbrook

The memorial was opened by Gundula Holbrook at a ceremony on 7 June 1997.

Next to the submarine is an award-winning café at which we had an excellent and reasonably priced lunch. The range of imaginative dishes on the menu was surprising and the food we ate was some of the best of the trip.

A quick look at the map suggested Tumut would be a good place to stop for the night, as it is effectively the northern tourist gateway to the Snowy Mountains.

This was nearly 90 miles away, giving a total distance for the day of just over 150 miles – our longest day.

We stayed in a very attractive site next to the River Tumut.

Having settled in, Jim, Alice and I went for a walk around town and thought that it looked very pretty, it had a surprising number of pubs, clubs and restaurants.

There was a fine sunset, after which we decided to eat out in town, rather than making our own meal.

HOLBROOK SHIRE COUNCIL
"OTWAY"

DEDICATED AS A TRIBUTE TO ALL SUBMARINERS
PAST, PRESENT AND FUTURE
UNVEILED BY
MRS GUNDULA HOLBROOK
WIDOW OF COMMANDER N.D. HOLBROOK V.C., R.N.
AFTER WHOM THIS TOWN IS NAMED
SATURDAY 7TH JUNE 1997

MAYOR JOAN I. PARKER

HMAS OTWAY
HOLBROOK NSW
Adopted Home of the Australian Submarine Squadron

Holbrook Submarine Museum Hologra

THE BOOT INN •WATCH BANDS
& BATTERIES
•GIFTWARE

KEY CUTTING

Boot & Saddlery - Repairs

WATCH
BATTERIES BOOT INN
REPLAC...

HOT

Telstra

P 1P

BL 36 EP

On this occasion, rather than walking, we unhitched the Kombi from its awning and drove up to town.

On the way out of the campsite we received a chorus of cheers and waves from some of the campers, who had earlier come over to have a look at, and talk about, the 'Cool Kombi'.

We left, hoping to find some good food, unhitching the Kombi from its awning and parking in the town centre only to find that every restaurant we had seen earlier was either closed, or empty of customers.

Possibly, April is too late in the season for Tumut tourists. We ended up in the rear dining room of one of the several two storey Victorian pubs, where we had a very decent meal served by a friendly and amusing waitress.

Day 13
Tumut to Jerrabomberra

The final day of our trip began with the inevitable visit to the local airfield, which proved to be fairly quiet, but in a beautiful setting with a mountain backdrop.

The first hangar we visited revealed a Sunbird two seat parasol monoplane and a Drifter microlight on floats.

Elsewhere on the field there was a very smart tailwheel Skyfox that was for sale – a snip at $35,000.

A Cessna 172 was parked on the apron.

All-in-all, the airfield looked like an idyllic location from which to fly.

Recreational Skyfox aircraft at Tumut

(Top) A Cessna 172 against the attractive Tumut backdrop

(Bottom) The rolling terrain between Tumut and Gundagi

From here we travelled on the hilly and winding cross-country road to Gundagai, with very attractive scenery. From there, we travelled the back to Jerrabomberra via Yass, arriving at 1:35 p.m.

The day's route formed the shape of an inverted horseshoe around the northern end of the Brindabella Mountains, covering a road distance of 210 km (132 miles).

Overall, the trip covered around 2,000 km (1,350 miles) in 13 days and the pre-planned route proved to be full of interest (except, perhaps, for the resolutely flat Murray River Highway).

The route is sketched opposite, running first North-East towards Goulburn, and then South-West through Canberra and Gundagai and broadly West out to Deniliquin and Swan Hill, returning in a broadly similar path.

Along the way this broad trail was enlivened by side trips to The Big Hole, Micalong Creek, Temora and Tumut, and, of course, the magnificent Antique Aircraft fly-in at Echuca.

From my perspective, this was a wonderful trip.

I particularly enjoyed not only the event at Echuca, but also the unexpected sights.

Who would have anticipated a submarine at Holbrook, or the sweet shop at Braidwood, let alone the beautiful bridges at Gundagai?

The echidna was an unexpected surprise, matched by an opportunity to see duck billed platypus in the wild, later in my visit.

I felt that this road trip gave a real feeling for the area and the variety of its sights and scenery.

I have to praise Jim for his careful driving and the Kombi for its almost faultless performance throughout and for providing such comfortable accommodation.

The Kombi was universally popular among those we met and we much appreciated the warmth with which we were received – not just at Echuca, but all along the route.

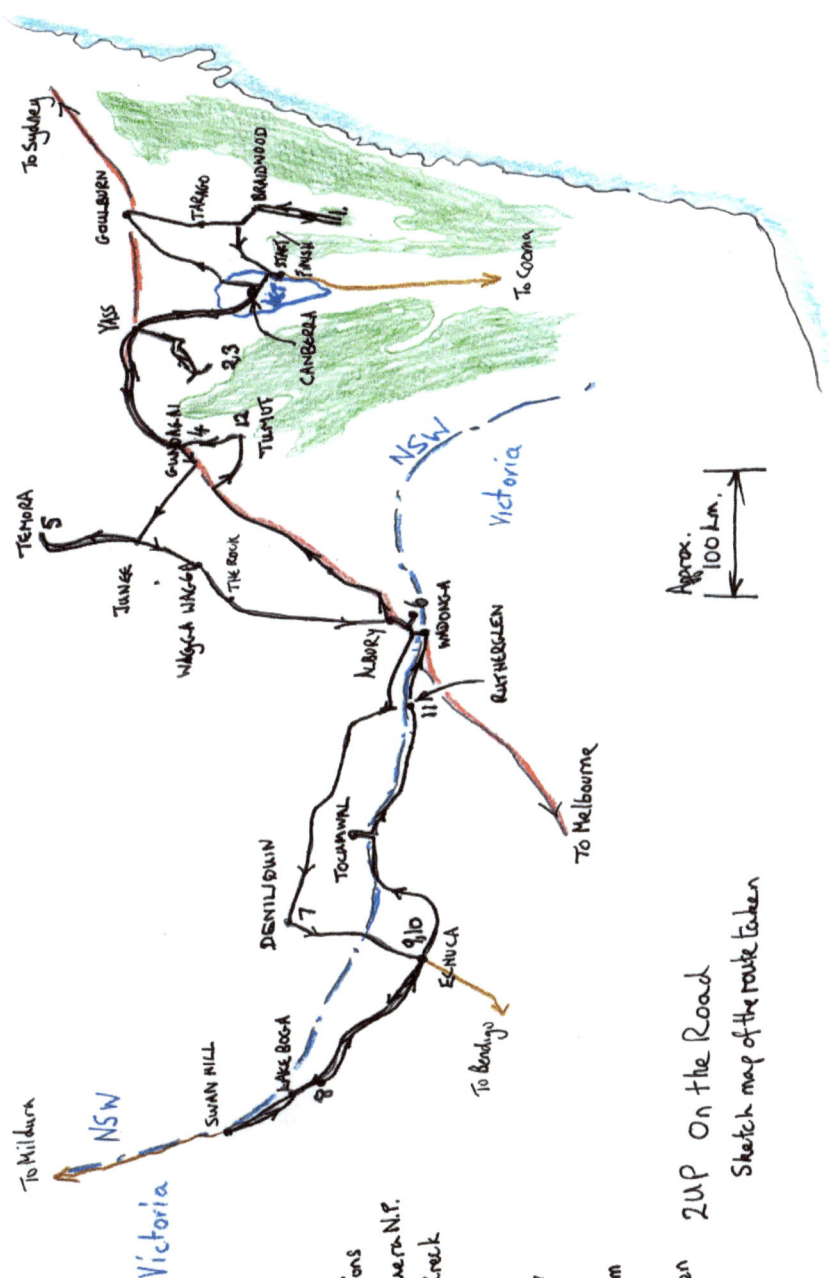

2UP On the Road
Sketch map of the route taken

Jim Smith

Postscript
A Kombi Celebrates the Centenary of the Canberra

The Centenary of Canberra Rally was held on the 18th and 19th of October 2013. The rally route linked the ACT port of Jervis Bay with Canberra itself, and the rally was a celebration of the part played by the motor car in the development of Canberra.

Alongside the rally a whole series of other 'Wheel-related' events were held over 'SPIN weekend'. I participated in the rally with my 1967 type 2 split-screen Kombi, which was built in Germany, exported to England and converted to be a Canterbury-Pitt camper.

I brought this vehicle to Australia some 11 years ago and have attended many club events since moving to Canberra in 2007.

Thanks to club member Brendan Jones for the opportunity to participate in what proved to be a fun event.

The rally start in Jervis Bay was reserved for a few cars because the organisers (and police) considered that the crossing of the Princes Highway by large numbers of old and slow vehicles would be too hazardous.

The bulk of the full rally participants started from HMAS Albatross near Nowra, leaving at about 9am on the Saturday morning.

For a Canberra resident to make this start time, it was necessary to pre-position in Nowra, so Kris and I set off on the Friday and drove down to Nowra following the rally route in reverse.

Shortly after arriving at our motel we had an inkling of the quality of the cars on the rally when we were joined at our motel by a beautiful red 1935 MG. This car had just been restored in WA, and had been brought over to the East coast in a container, specifically to participate in the rally and for the owners to spend a holiday in the mountains.

When parked up next to the Kombi, the quality of the MG restoration was readily apparent, and this car went on to be judged the best pre-1939 car at the rally.

Having taken the worst of the bugs off the Kombi on the Friday night, we made a fairly early start in the morning and headed up to Albatross for the drivers' briefing and to check out the other cars on the rally. We also made our own preparations for the event – drivers and crew were invited to dress in any style appropriate to the rally, and inevitably we travelled in suitable 60s attire, eventually winning a prize for best-dressed 60s and 70s.

At the start the cars were grouped by age, and one of the photos shows one of the lines of 50s and 60s cars.

The more modern cars left first because the route from HMAS Albatross up to the first checkpoint at Tarago featured some steep and windy roads. In the event, everything progressed smoothly. The run developed into a convoy of mixed marques and ages progressing at about 70 kph up the climb to Nerriga, and then up again to Tarago.

The road was a little narrow and had some short, steep stretches, requiring a shift to 2nd gear on two occasions. There was one stretch of about 1.5km of well-graded dirt road but, in general, a smooth journey was made. At Tarago, the rally stopped for morning tea, for another drivers' briefing, and to get the rally passport stamped to record our progress.

Some 100 additional cars joined the rally at Tarago, some of which were too precious to have risked the journey up the hill from Nowra.

The town put on a fine welcome and a brunch for participants, and the stop also provided an opportunity to look around, both at the new participants at Tarago and at those that had travelled with us.

There were a few Beetles, including one towing a matching caravan, but no other Kombis.

From Tarago, the Rally followed gently-rolling roads for 30 km or so, to Bungendore, where there was another compulsory stop.

At Bungendore, the rally was joined by a number of the older cars from the Canberra area, and there was another opportunity to have some refreshments and get the rally card stamped. Another addition to the Rally at Bungendore was a recently restored bay window Kombi, accompanied in this picture by the ACT Government's Nissan electric car, which was used the next day to lead the Rally down to Old Parliament House.

After refreshments at Bungendore, the trip back to Canberra via Queanbeyan was straightforward.

Participants made their way to overnight accommodation, or to the excellent SPIN program of events laid on to coincide with the rally.

The evening events included a spectacular fashion show with all the garments made from car parts, presented in an entertainingly burlesque style, a trapeze act, and the Petrosexuals fronted by Mark Seymour (Hunters and Collectors) playing an excellent set of motoring rock.

Next day, all made their way to the Exhibition Park in Canberra (EPIC) to parade in convoy down to the lawns of Old Parliament House. At EPIC, the numbers were further swelled by cars joining for the very short run down to the City Centre and across the lake to park-up.

Highlights were the good turn-out of pre-1930 cars, strong contingent of American and Aussie muscle cars, many old favourites, and the number of participants dressed for the occasion.

The oldest car in the rally was a 101 year-old Overlander. There were also a number of participants less than a decade old.

In the evening, after the Rally, there was a gala dinner at the National Museum of Australia and the winners of the Concours competition were announced. In addition to the 1935 MG, the prizes were awarded to a Citroen DS and a BMW Isetta bubble car.

The Canterbury-Pitt Kombi

Overnight in Nowra with a 1935 MG for company

Dressing the part 'Ozzie and Shazza' a.k.a. Jim and Kris

ROAD SUBJECT TO
FLOODING
INDICATORS SHOW DEPTH

The Wild One

GT

36·908

(Top) Beautiful red E-type Jaguar at Tarago for morning tea

(Bottom) Beetle and its matching teardrop caravan

(Top) Magnificent Salmson

(Bottom) Healey 3000, Porsche & Kombi;

(Top) The growing Rally fleet at Bungendore

(Bottom) Beautifully restored bay-window camper and the ACT Government's electric car, Bungendore

(Top) The 101 year old Overlander at EPIC, the oldest car in the rally;
(Bottom) Magnificent pre-war Chrysler at EPIC

(Top) Ford Mustang, also at Tarago; (Bottom) The Kombi's rally passport stamped at HMAS Albatross, Tarago, Bungendore, EPIC and Old Parliament House

CENTENARY OF CANBERRA RALLY

NAME James Smith

VEHICLE VW Type 2

MAKE VOLKSWAGEN

REGISTRATION BA710D

YEAR 1967

CENTENARY OF CANBERRA RALLY
ITINERARY

Day 1. Saturday 19 October

7.00am Selected vehicles arrive Jervis Bay for ceremonial start

7.15 Driver briefing at Jervis Bay

7.15 HMAS Albatross is opened to participants' vehicles. Support vehicles will admitted to the base if registration and passengers details are submitted to Office prior to October 18 as HMAS Albatross is a secure, operational naval

7.15 Registration open and rally pack collection at HMAS Albatross

7.30 Start Jervis Bay. Vehicles flagged off by Mick Gentleman MLA

8.00 Jervis Bay vehicles arrive at HMAS Albatross

8.00 Driver briefing HMAS Albatross

8.10 Event main start HMAS Albatross

10.00 Gates open for vehicles starting at Tarago. Entry to the Rally site for parti will be from Lumley Rd in Tarago, with backup vehicle and public parking on Braidwood Road. Site maps will be provided in packs and marshals will vehicles once in Tarago. Only rally vehicles will be admitted to the site.

10.00 Morning tea/brunch, registration and rally packs available at Tarago

10.05 Vehicles start arriving from HMAS Albatross at Tarago Recreation Reserve

10.45 Driver briefing Tarago

11.00 Start - Tarago

11.30 First vehicles arrive in Frog's Hollow, Bungendore. Drivers will do a loop Bungendore before entering Frog's Hollow. Event marshals will guide drive route will be sign posted.

11.30 Registration desk/pack collection/passport stamp open at Frog's Hollow

12.00 Rally participants have a break for lunch, entertainment, and activities p Bungendore before proceeding to Canberra

2.00pm onwards SPIN events Canberra www.spinweekend.com.au

5.00 - 7.00 SPIN Twilight. At 255 Canberra Avenue, Fyshwick, Canberra

7.00 - 10.00 SPIN Adults Only. 255 Canberra Avenue.

Day 2. Sunday 20 October

7.30am Gates open for participants, kits, registration and passport stamps

8.30 Driver briefing

8.45 Official Start. Speech and flag start by Chief Minister ACT, Katie Gallagher

8.50 Australian Federal Police escorted Centenary Rally Cruise to Old Parliam Escorted by modern and vintage police vehicles to OPH for the following:

10.00 Breakfast/morning tea for drivers. Catered by Marymead

1.30 Concours d'Elegance judging

6.30 - 10pm Gala Dinner. Main Hall, National Museum of Australia.

(Top) The Concours d'Elegance competitors on the lawns at the Old Parliament House

(Bottom) Ferraris, at Tarago

Pages 234 - 239 - A last look round

Image Index

Canterbury Pitt comes to Canberra

Up Again

Two Up On The Road

170 (Top) Chinese Nanchang CJ6 aerobatic trainer VH-NNC

(Bottom) Two NZAI CT/4s flew in to Echuca

171 (Top) VH-ROA is a 1949 Stinson 108-3 Voyager

(Bottom) Thorp T-18 homebuilt VH-WSJ

172 Warren Canning's Van's RV6 with Jim on board

174 Paddle steamer Emmylou on the Murray River at Echuca

177 (Top) An 1951 Auster J/1B Aiglet VH-WAZ

(Bottom) The Avro Cadet had a busy day

178 (Top) The rare 1934 British Aircraft Klemm Eagle VH-UTI

(Bottom) 1952 Cessna Birddog VH-UXX taking off

179 (Top) 1940 Commonwealth CA-3 Wirraway VH-WWY at Echuca

(Bottom) Fine action shot of Winjeel VH-HFM stirring up the dust on the taxiway

180 An immaculate DH82A Tiger Moth VH-NWM

182 (Top) VH-UTV (painted as A33-1)

(Bottom) An Immaculate 1947 DHC-1 Chipmunk VH-MCC

183 (Top) An Luscombe 8A operating on the recreation aircraft register as 24-5184

(Bottom) A 1941 Ryan ST-3 KR VH-RPT

184 The magnificent 1939 WACO AGC-8 NC66206

186 Tuffy and Tippy heaven

187 The red gum 'log buggy' in Echuca

188 The going-away car

191 (Top) Unexpected visitor SIAI Marchetti S-211 VH-DZJ

(Bottom) Tocumwal, Schleiche ASW-15B glider, the Sportavia hangar is in the background

192 Scheibe Bergfalke training glider

194 The only two Pascoe EP2 gliders in the hangar at Tocumwal

196 homebuilt Stratus, Tocumwal

198 Glider advert for Sportavia

199 A Wingless Pawnee at Yarrawonga

200 sinister trees, Lake Mulwalla

200 Man-made lake, Rutherglen

201 Lake at Rutherglen campsite

203 Sapphire microlight on a pole in Holbrook

204 HMAS Otway, Holbrook and Memorial Dedication plaque

206 Royal Hotel Tumut

208 Another of Tumut's fine pubs

210 Beautiful River Tumut

211 Sunset Tumut

212 Recreational Skyfox aircraft at Tumut

213 (Top) A Cessna 172 against the attractive Tumut backdrop

(Bottom) Rolling terrain of Tumut and Gundagi

214 The winding road towards the slopes of the Brindabellas

217 The Route

A Kombi Celebrates The Centenary of the Canberra

Ron & Jim Smith

'Two Up' is a collection of aviation anecdotes and photographs going back to the brothers' early fascination with aircraft in the sixties. It includes a wealth of inside information. From the sixties both Smith brothers have spent their life, leisure and working time in and around an industry that has seen phenomenal changes over the last fifty years.

Ron Smith has had a long and varied association with aviation. He is an aerospace engineer, a Fellow of the Royal Aeronautical Society, ex-Chairman of the Royal Aeronautical Society Rotorcraft Committee, author of aviation books and articles, aircraft owner, private pilot and aviation photographer. After 15 years at Westland Helicopters & 22 years with British Aerospace / BAE Systems, Ron's books include the 5 volume *British Built Aircraft* series (The History Press); *Cessna 172: A Pocket History* & *Piper Cherokee: A Family History* (Amberley Publishing); *Classic Light Aircraft*, & *Twin Cessna*, (Schiffer Publishing).

Jim Smith recently retired from a senior management position after 14 years at the Australian Defence Science and Technology Group. Trained as an aeronautical engineer, he has BSc and Masters degrees from the University of Southampton, UK. Before moving to Australia, Jim worked for the UK Ministry of Defence (MoD) for 28 years. His experience includes involvement with a wealth of British and Australian research and major defence projects, many of which were with international partners.

9781908135391 SECOND EDITION
9781908135445 eBook

www.ingramcontent.com/pod-product-compliance
Lightning Source LLC
Chambersburg PA
CBHW040939100426
42812CB00015B/2622